No Place To Lie

Helen Garlick

For my family, my tribe.

Foreword

30th January 2018

A still sunrise is soon to break over the village of Brill in Buckingham-shire, on a blue day sharpened by diamond frost. Largely red brick, Brill sits high on a round hill along the upward English curve which divides stone houses from brick, the placid Cotswolds on the west separating away from the hardworking Midlands to the east.

Brill has a history of keeping mum.

> *I went to Noke*
> *And nobody spoke.*
> *I went to Brill*
> *They were silent still.*

The sun will take longer to light up this west-facing bedroom window of our Airbnb house overlooking the village green. A brave shrub of winter flowering honeysuckle sits by the front door and its fragrance whispers in through the window, lifting winter's chill. A blackbird, Gregory Porter of garden birds, is fluting out his heart on the pear tree outside, although spring is weeks away. Perhaps it's a serenade for Mum.

Nestled next to the man I am due to marry this summer, a second chance for each of us, feelings of peace – and, in truth, relief – are unfurling after the drama of my mother's death before Christmas. While Tim sleeps, I twist a ring around on the little finger of my right hand, before lifting my hand out from under the duvet to look at it as the sun leans into the day. The ring holds a small, milky, oval opal in a raised gold frame. Its gold band is adjustable to fit any finger. Familiar, unfathomable, flashing pink, blue, turquoise depending on how the light falls, the opal flickers red when it touches skin. I have known my mother's ring for as long as I can remember. No one ever told me who gave it to her: most likely it was my father.

Today is Mum's funeral. My sun-worshipping mother died on the shortest winter day, when the sun has its least power. 'She wouldn't have felt a thing,' the coroner advised me. 'It would be like a light being switched off.' Her heart gave out unexpectedly, eight days after her admission into care, her much-loved freedom docked. This begins a time when I hope I can also lay to rest the ghost of the 'accident' of my brother David's death, and speak more openly about how his life ended.

You are only as sick as your secrets, so they say. I have been trying to heal myself from the secrets of my past for a long time now. But my mum's confession about being 'afflicted' (sadly, her choice of word) which she handwrote on the back of a white envelope, left to be found by me after her death, means I will carry another secret for a while longer. This one none of us even suspected, whereas everyone really knew what had happened to David.

I don't want her funeral to be about the envelope. I want her day to be about the life she decided to lead with my father for the nearly fifty-nine years they were married until the day he died; about her being a doting grandmother; about the grand houses they lived in, their travel, setting up the Doncaster Film Club, the theatre, parties and conviviality they loved. The things she was proud of, including being a mother. I owe her that.

My mother said it was important to get things right. Black for funerals. I'll be draped in midnight from my platform suede shoes to a glossy feathered hat, with a veil part covering my face – she would approve of the veil. Apart from my lips, which I'll paint red to celebrate life, the only colour on me will be her opal ring.

I silently practise the first line of the eulogy I plan to give later this morning.

'I am and will always not be the same but be different.'

This is how she began her handwritten confession. I won't read any more from it at the funeral; the time for that will be later.

•

In the meantime, how can I begin to unravel the truths hidden within my family of origin; shrouded by secrets for so long? I'm aware that I simply do not know how much I don't know, but then maybe that's true for everyone. In childhood, normal is whatever normally happens.

We could start with the day that changed everything, which still cuts deep. Nobody could say that what happened on that day was anything like normal.

My younger daughter, with clear-eyed teenage wisdom, once said, 'Stuff happens, Mum.' Stuff. Who could argue with that? When we're young we know so much. Then we have to forget when we're grown up, in order to get by.

I won't pretend that the stuff covered in this book is easy reading. If you choose to turn away, you wouldn't be the first. People have crossed the road to avoid speaking to me in the past. I can't blame them.

If you are carrying on reading, you might like to figure out why this stuff did happen. I won't be able to give you all the answers; there are things that I don't know even now. My family begat more questions than answers. I would hazard a guess that you'll identify more of the causes than I have, even though I've spent nearly forty years puzzling it out.

I am writing this book now to keep a promise I made to myself back in 1981. The most important promises are those you make inside. If you can't trust yourself, how can you trust anyone else?

For those brave enough to read on: thank you. I will use my best endeavours to explain what happened. That's a term in law, by the way, 'best endeavours'. I could instead say 'undertake', which is a higher legal test. But I don't honestly know what was going on inside others, only myself. And I'm not even certain that is accurate. I'll stick with best endeavours.

I don't want to make a promise I might break. There's been enough of that already.

Part One
A Beginning

Live as long as you may, the first twenty years
are the longest half of your life.
Robert Southey

Foxes have holes, and birds have nests,
but the son of man has no place to lie down and rest.
Luke 9:58

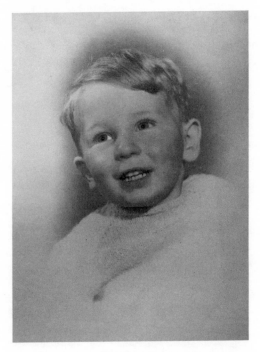

David, aged 2

Chapter 1

1st March 1981: St David's Day

If anyone had asked me about my family then, I would have said there were four of us, although that would no longer be the truth. We could have been five, but my little sister died before she took a breath. Today, which happens to be a Sunday, we are down to three.

If you could see through a gap in the closed curtains of the green room of Bothamsall Hall, Nottinghamshire, you might detect a black bakelite telephone on the floor next to the settee, receiver askew from the cradle. Near the phone, also on the floor, is a lamp knocked over, its shade broken away from the base. Next to the settee lies my younger brother David, not quite twenty-one years old, on the black and red carpet, his unseeing eyes still wide open. The Russian shotgun, containing one spent cartridge, is shielded from sight by his body. It is held in David's left hand, pointing towards what was his temple. Fragments of my little brother trace an arc from his head upwards to the wall and ceiling in the room where he took his last breath the day before. Or it could have been the day before that, or even earlier.

The overhead lights and the television are on and have not been switched off for several days. No one has been bothered enough by this to check what's going on. Nobody has knocked at the door in the last week to see if he is all right. This is about to change.

My father Geoffrey swings his automatic burgundy Daimler through the gate pillars, ignoring the 'Private' sign, and over the driveway of Bothamsall Hall, to pull up by a yellow Renault 5 hatchback where the car purrs to a stop. He places the gear lever in park, slips on the hand brake, and looks at his watch: 4 p.m. The drive up from London has been long. Quickly checking his reflection in the mirror, he threads a greying strand of hair across his balding head, while thinking about his son. He allows himself a momentary hope that this time things will be easy between them.

After the dusting of snow a few days ago, it is unseasonably mild. A drizzle mists over the scene as grey light fades into dusk. He is reluctant to step into the cold outside, but he has his duty to do. He looks across at his wife, sitting in the passenger seat beside him.

'I'll pop in to see if David's tidied things up before you come in,' Geoffrey says. 'Look – the lights are on inside, and I think I can hear the telly. It's a blasted nuisance the phone's not working. Fault on the line, the operator said, if you believe that. You stay here, Monica, in the warm. I won't be long.'

My parents have just come back from a holiday in Cyprus, to get away from this English winter, top up the tans. It's the first holiday abroad they've had this year and it won't be the last. Rolling stones, Geoffrey and Monica, that's what people say. Always going from this place to that, one home to another. He likes it that way; it makes life interesting.

She doesn't answer, but nods and turns away from him to look at the garden, still awash with leaves from autumn, drifting in clumps under the trees and hedges where the wind has blown them. That needs clearing up, she thinks. She wants to get out of the car and see her son David, her younger child, as soon as she can. She's missed him on holiday. But she's not overly fond of Cleo, the Gordon setter he's looking after for her daughter – or any dog, come to that. So she obeys and perches herself back in her seat. She exhales extra heavily to tell Geoffrey that he is making her do this.

Her husband pushes himself out of the car, slams the door harder than he meant to, and walks towards the house, past the yellow hatchback, brushing his hand on the bonnet. Stone cold. The shadows are darkening but in the boot he can still spot dog food – at least twenty tins of Chappie, as well as several yellow and red bags of Pedigree dog biscuits. That's pretty odd. He checks the car doors, all locked, before walking around to the front of the Hall. No sign of his son here. He rings the front door-bell and hears its chimes echoing in the hall. Geoffrey has his own key to the front door but that's in the safe in his Doncaster office. He tsks in irritation. After a pause he rings again, this time for longer. Still no answer. He turns on his heel to retrace his steps and walks around to the back door.

He finds it shut, but with a key fob made with a wooden cotton-reel bobbin, which he doesn't recognise, hanging from the lock, the bobbin attached with coloured wool to the heavy metal key and waving slightly in a gust of air. He has to knock as the doorbell hasn't worked for a few weeks now. David really should have fixed that. Apart from the sound of the TV, or maybe a radio, all he hears is silence. Not even a dog barking, or howling at the moon as Cleo is sometimes prone to do. And there is no response to his knocking.

He might be walking the dog, Geoffrey tells himself. Or maybe he's on the loo. Holding his breath, he cranes to hear whether it's a radio – no, definitely the telly. He tries the handle of the door, which opens before he even needs to twist round the key from which the bobbin dangles down. The door catches slightly on the floor beneath, so he has to thrust it harder before it opens enough to let him in. As he steps into the door, he sees a packed bag and a neat pile of David's belongings, carefully ordered, in the hall, as if his son is ready to go.

'David?' he calls out. Still no answer. Taking a deep breath to make his shout louder, he feels a chill biting into his lungs. It seems colder inside than out. Why hasn't he put the central heating on? Perhaps he wants to cut down on bills for the owner? Well he didn't really need to do that, Geoffrey thinks. The owner is well off, I should know, he's my client, and he's lucky to have my son look after this pile whilst he's away.

Geoffrey makes his way to the green room to check if his twenty-year-old son is asleep in there.

•

Outside in the car, Monica sets her navy blue leather handbag down on her lap, unzipping the pouch underneath the flap to take out her diary and her Sunkiss lipstick, placed just there, like always. She pulls down the sun visor to check her face before carefully painting the curved bow of her lips, first the bottom and then the top lip, smiling as she catches the glint of her opal ring on her right hand in the mirror. She squeezes and rubs her lips together to even the colour out, an elegant shade of peach, not at all common. Not baby pink, like her younger sister Judy might go for.

The shape of Monica's lipstick is the exact moulded contour of her mouth. She can put on lipstick pretty much with her eyes closed, even without a mirror, and she sometimes does, at the table at the end of a dinner party before the dancing starts. She gives a faint smile to herself in the reflection of the mirror, looking at the freckles on her face from the Cypriot sun, her high cheekbones, cornflower blue eyes, before her face rests back into the stillness she normally wears.

She opens up her diary to make a note in biro, straining to see the page. *1st March. Check with Bill – Cleo? Dog food? Phone mother. Butchers Tues. 1lb of mince, 2-3 chicken legs? ½ doz. eggs.*

Monica plans to have her son over for a meal at 13 Albion Place. She likes to see him as much as she can, preferably on Wednesdays, it breaks the week up a bit. Usually she and Geoffrey go to Bothamsall but it would be nice to cook for David at home this time. She could do his favourite, spaghetti Bolognese, with grated parmesan if she's got some. He'll have to bring that dog, I suppose, she sighs. But if Geoffrey says that we can't have spaghetti Bolognese as it's too messy, I'll suggest we have chicken legs instead. Geoffrey doesn't like legs, he only likes breasts, so that might mean he'd opt for Bolognese. Her lips move into a slight smile. That will work and Geoffrey will think it's his idea.

She wakes up from her reverie: Geoffrey is tapping on the car window.

'Monica, Monica.'

He says her name over and over. She winds the window down and sees her husband's green eyes are wet, his pupils black holes. His face is ashen. She watches him for the seconds it takes him to find some words. Geoffrey always knows what to say. What on earth is wrong with him?

'Don't come out. Stay in the car,' he stammers. 'I don't know what's happened. There must have been an accident. Or there's been an intruder. But you mustn't come in. You can't. We can't touch anything or move anything although I'm going to have a look around. We'll have to wait for the police. I've already called 999, and they're heading straight over.'

Rebelliously, she moves to open the door handle, but her husband pushes the door back firmly, leaning against it with his whole weight. He clears his throat to speak more authoritatively, like he usually does.

'No. Listen to me, Monica. Don't come in. It could be the death of you. Don't move. Stay right here, you promise me? Wait until I come back.'

Monica sinks back in her seat, suddenly sapped of strength. She nods her head again but this time again watches her husband like a hawk as he heads back inside the Hall, forcing her eyelids open, not blinking, to work out for herself what is going on. What has happened to her golden boy?

Chapter 2

This may or may not be the truth of what happened. I was not at Bothamsall Hall, together with what was left of my family. Although 'together' would be misleading: there were spaces between us, not connections. Silences were familiar territory; my homeland.

A version of the facts became the family story, as I recall it, of the agony of my father discovering my brother's body, pieced together from my parents' clues as well as my imagination. Sometimes my parents alluded to a bit of what had happened; occasionally they might have said 'I said …', or 'You said …', and told me something they may or may not have said. I've included in this book scenes in the voices of each of the four main characters, which you could say wouldn't be the truth, but I've tried to be as true as I can, with my current 2020 vision, to the spirit of what happened. Where I later find out that what really happened is different from how I remembered it, I've tried to cover that in Part Three. I've also changed some names and other details to protect the privacy of people still alive. But I don't want to mislead you: that's not my intention.

I've usually had to figure things out on my own.

You never knew quite where you were with my mother. She kept herself hidden. I loved her – babies are primed to love their mothers – and of course she loved me. She had told me that, and it ought to be true.

Our family's story, probably most of this book, will be a lot about my mother, who didn't like her own mother although she would never confess it. Instead, she loved her father's mother, who ran a haberdashery shop in Doncaster on her own after she'd sent her husband out to get some supplies from Leeds when it was bitter, snowing, in the bleak midwinter, and he'd died of the flu after. My mother and her father's mother, her Nana, were one of a kind. Mummy didn't love many people in her life, although she must have loved herself, and she later became a devoted grannie, just like her mother before her.

My mum's name was Monica but everyone in the family, except her husband, called her Pip because she was the apple of her daddy's eye. The mirror-pool of Pip's world mostly reflected back just the still face of Pip. Her death proved to be the only end to her outrage towards Aunty Judy, seven years younger than her, for the capital error of being born.

Monica Nicholson, known as Pip, aged 8

'They promised me that I would always be the only one. It devastated me when Judy came along.' My mother's record kept playing this track until she died, often recounting the tale of when she had been sent out to take her sister for a walk and they came back on opposite sides of the road. I couldn't understand it when I was little. Aunty Judy was everything my mother wasn't: giggly, fun-loving, energetic, enthusiastic, warm. Everyone loved Aunty Judy, especially my grannie. We laughed more when Judy was around.

My mother taught me a lot, but not the usual stuff you get to mention in Mother's Day cards. There was more than a whisper of magic about her. She offered, for example, to teach me self-control, so that people wouldn't be able to read me.

'I taught myself not to blush when I was a girl. I could teach you how to do that too, if you're interested. It comes in useful. You just have to look at yourself in a mirror, imagine something which makes you go red and then make the blood drain away from your face.'

She taught me things which were hard to talk about with other people: how not to be the favourite, how to be the one who sorts things out, how to see what happens in silence.

People said that my brother, my mother and her father were cut from the same stuff.

'All fair. That blond, blue-eyed gene goes from father to daughter to son, hops from female to male and back again, all the way down the generations. It was the same with your grandfather's mother, Helen. Cold as Christmas, she was. She never could stand me. And another thing,' she added. 'They don't talk much either.'

She was dead right about that. That was my grandmother, Madge, my mother's mother, talking. Marjorie Nicholson, née Tyler, one of the proud Tyler women, wasn't sleety. She was frisky sometimes, schoolmistressy the next minute, then singing 'My Blue Heaven' and making me hot buttered toast with her homemade raspberry jam after that. At Palace Farm, she grew sensitive plants in her greenhouse, the ones which shrink when you touch them, and she had goldfish in her pond which were slimy on your fingers, and strawberries and pea pods in the garden. They were too delicious, making your mouth water just thinking about picking them. She taught me that I was strong, a Tyler woman just like her.

I loved Grannie Madge more than anyone else in the world. In 1920, aged nineteen, she'd studied French for a year at the Sorbonne in Paris as part of her degree at Sheffield University. It was wonderful to have a grannie who'd broken barriers to get a university degree and become a teacher of deaf children, like a better class of fairy story.

And my grandfather used to do tricks! He – Les, short for Lesley – was an engineer, working on the railways in the day, and in his spare time he made things. He carved us stilts and toboggans out of wood for Christmas presents. They said he was a member of The Magic Circle, although he never told me that himself. He used to dress up in a top hat and tails

Madge Nicholson, London Zoo

and be a proper magician at my parties – sometimes even at David's parties. My grandpa (who went bald at twenty-one, but Grannie Madge fell in love with him because he could dance like Fred Astaire) would swallow fire and carve goldfish out of carrots, and then pretend to eat a real goldfish and we would all go 'Euurgh!' and he would slightly smile, and give me a tiny wink, but not so much that anyone else would notice. Vivienne, my friend from school, was actually sick at that, and Mummy had to take her out of the drawing room with a look on her face and telephone her mother to take her home.

'We're never going to have that wretched girl over again if she has to be sick all the time,' my mother said to me, although not to Vivienne nor her mummy, and Vivienne had actually only been sick once before at our house. But that's what happened. She couldn't come over anymore. I had to pretend I didn't know why Mummy didn't let me invite her back again, and eventually she stopped being my friend.

I tried never to be sick in front of my parents. They didn't like it.

Most people believe that others think like them. But my father was a rebel, following Sheffield Wednesday when the rest of his family followed United; aiming high to go to Cambridge and read classics, the first in his family, apart from his cousin Peter, to go to university. He only went there because his headmaster told his parents he would have to work harder than any miner if he got into Cambridge. He was funny, sometimes kind and took many things seriously: he was firmly opposed to capital punishment when almost everyone else believed it was right. I was enough of a rebel to be able to cope with his expectation that testing us would bring out our strength – his fire forging our steel. Arguably, that worked for me, but not so much for David.

My father was born and brought up in Sheffield. Ambitious, clever, musical without ever having played a musical instrument (his parents didn't bring him up to do that, so he was a listener rather than a player). He had an older brother, Jimmy, the funniest man I think I've ever known and also one of the kindest, who later married Kathleen, the perfect warm, loving mother. I loved spending time with them and their two children, Richard and Alison, but we didn't get to do that much.

My Nana, Dad's Scottish mother, talked too much and irritated almost everyone, including my father with whom she was obsessed.

'My little Geoffrey. He was so precious. I used to dress him up in a little peach suit and show him off to everyone. Such a bonnie baby.'

Peach? In Sheffield? In the thirties? Too much. She ended her life in a Sheffield hospital with stomach cancer, morphined to the gills yet still terrified. Nana used to look after David more at weekends, when we got older, whereas I still got to stay with my dancing grannie. The

Geoffrey Garlick, Sidney Sussex College,
Cambridge. Graduation photograph

logic of this was that Nana knew about boys having had sons and Grannie knew about girls having had daughters. But when we were little, David and I both got to stay with Grannie and Grandpa. The happiest time I can remember was when Aunty Judy and Uncle Tony came over to Palace Farm, and put Judy's son Ricky and me on their shoulders and we 'cantered' around in the field, charging each other in circles and laughing so much my sides hurt. I hung on to that memory like gold dust.

My brother David, two years and one month younger, didn't have many parties. That was mostly because it was a lot of effort and David didn't like to have to try too hard with other people. He liked an uncomplicated life, so he could collect birds' eggs, glue up balsa wood Spitfires, count how many seconds it took for Action Man to fall from the window or look up at the stars through his telescope. Later on everything was metallic: he put on iron armour to be Ivanhoe, graduating to motocross bikes and then heavy metal music. When he was little you could hardly get into his bedroom, there were so many twiggy nests, hanging planes, homemade parachutes, fragile shells, fishing lines and all his treasures.

I wasn't like that. I didn't want to collect things and not have parties. I wanted to explore the world, read books, write, have intense, deep conversations, seize life with both hands. I daydreamed things out in my favourite hidey-place, under the willow tree in the garden. I was clever and a bit impatient, more like my father. I ended up being a solicitor like him, though I didn't go to Cambridge, or play hockey or table tennis, and I wasn't President of the Yorkshire Union of Law Societies like he was for donkey's years. As I got older, I looked more like my mother. My mum had corn-gold hair, with slight red flecks. If she left it her hair went wild, so she was always trying to tame it. My mum was a beauty, everyone knew that too, and they even told me so. There could be no doubt about it.

I knew from an early age that there was something not being said. When I was four years old, when we lived in the old red brick rectory in Tickhill, I came back in from playing with Treever, our golden retriever, in the garden. I didn't know there was a party going on, caught up in my own world, skipping into the drawing room from the sun-hot garden outside. I opened the heavy wooden door, surprised to see so many grown-ups behind it. Their laughter and chatter died as soon as they noticed me and they went quiet. That was not the only time. I knew there was something going on – a secret – I just didn't know what it was. I thought it was maybe because I was adopted, but my search through the red leather oval hatbox with the broken lid which contained their documents yielded no adoption papers. Clearly I was theirs, even though I didn't fit in. I dreamed of one day finding a place where I felt properly at home, with my own family, my tribe.

As a child, I was pretty sure that Marhamchurch in North Cornwall, where we used to go every holiday, was really only about, I don't know, twenty miles away, although it could have been as much as fifty, but to prove it was a holiday rather than just a trip to the fish market in Donny which they said was only seven miles away, they would drive around and around for eight hours before we arrived at our destination. The Salt Box, Marhamchurch, our family holiday home.

Motorways weren't built then so we had to drive down the Fosse Way, right through Lichfield. We had to get up early in the morning for the journey and we kept our pyjamas on to have a longer sleep. I didn't like Lichfield. Rows and rows of thirties houses in a long, straight line. It was always raining when we drove through Lichfield, which is about where we usually woke up. I used to think that if I had to live in a place called Lichfield in a house the same as all the others on a long straight road when I was grown-up, then I just didn't know how I could carry on living. I was in such a hurry to grow up and get away.

Chapter 3

Four thousand one hundred miles away, I am having lunch in St Louis, Missouri, hosted by Peter Davis, formerly a miner's son from Doncaster, now a professor at Wharton Business School, together with some of his friends, with whom I've been staying. I have just returned from Mexico, travelling with my old Bristol university friend Nicky. Soon I'll be heading to New Orleans on a paddle steamer, to arrive for Mardi Gras. Lunch is arranged in a restaurant overlooking the Mississippi River, with the gleaming steel Gateway Arch towering over the city in full view of the high, wide windows.

'You'd never have believed it. When the next bus came to collect the passengers from the first broken-down bus, we all got back on, chickens in cages, children, grannies, everyone, then stopped at two border patrols. At the second, the bus was about to leave without Nicky, still inside with the machine-gun armed guards. I channelled my inner Joyce Grenfell, told the driver, "I am a British citizen and so is my friend. You must wait for us!", rushed back into the border post, past the armed guards, picked up her suitcase and said "We're leaving". Amazingly, we got away and the bus driver hadn't driven off. What a narrow escape!' Safe now, among lovely people, I laugh at the memory, stripped of its fear.

As we finish coffee, Peter leans over and tells me quietly, 'We need to go into the next room. You need to take a private telephone call.'

His friends exchange glances.

'Your father wants to speak to you.'

'Why?' I ask. 'Have I done something wrong?'

'Goodness, no. Not at all, but you must take this call. Come with me, you'll – we'll – be private in here.'

A waiter leads the way and the two of us go into a side room. I feel uneasy, noticing a tightness in Peter's jawline.

The restaurant manager is already there, holding a telephone receiver, and bows his head slightly to Peter. 'Is he on the line?' asks Peter. The manager nods. Peter takes the phone handset and the manager discreetly leaves the room.

'Geoffrey, are you there? Can you hear me? Hello there.'

Dad must have said yes. What is going on?

'It's Peter. I won't stop on the phone very long as I have Helen here now. We've just had lunch. Helen can speak to you now. No, I haven't said anything to her yet.'

I take the receiver. There is no 'How are you?', no pleasantries. Why not? What does 'I haven't said anything to her yet' mean, precisely? What hasn't Peter told me?

'Daddy, how are you? And Mummy?' I'm using Mummy and Daddy rather than the more usual Mum and Dad. I feel guiltily bad that I have been so little in touch over the last few days, if not weeks. I sent a postcard from Bahía de Kino, I think. 'Is everything all right?'

The last time I received a call from my parents before 6 p.m. when the cheaper telephone rate kicks in was when my grandpa died in 1976. We are from Yorkshire. Judging by the time of the call, someone had died. That call about Grandpa had been kind of predictable – he'd smoked a lot. I remember with a stab of anguish the tragic death of a schoolfriend in a car accident when I was seventeen, that knocked us all for six, but that was years ago, he can't be calling about that. Maybe it's my grannie. Please not Grannie.

My father takes in a gulp of air which I can hear right across the Atlantic. His voice catches.

'Helen. My dearest Helen. I am afraid I have some news, very bad news. Your mother and I are here together. We think you will need to come back home soon, though that is up to you of course, if you want to continue your, your trip. We love you very much.'

'What is it, Daddy?' I say, then, 'Who is it? Who's died?' It can't be anything else.

'It's David,' my father says, with a sob. 'It's your brother.' He stops, and then says, 'So you see why we'd like you to come home now?'

Peter's hand touches my shoulder. I can't look back at him. I look at the floor.

'Yes, of course. Oh God.'

'There's been a terrible accident. David was at Bothamsall Hall, it's near Retford, as you know, not far away, looking after that wretched client's place, being the caretaker, helping him out, you know after he got let down by the other chap who was supposed to do it. Your mother and I were in Cyprus for a holiday and after we got back we couldn't get hold of David; the phone was out of order. So we drove over to Bothamsall. I found him, Helen. I called the ambulance and the police. 999. Nothing could be done by the ambulance, he'd gone already. The police came.' This came out in a rush.

'But what happened? Was there an accident? Had he fallen? Why did you need to call the police? Did he leave you a note or anything?'

'A note? No. Why? No, nothing like that. It'll be investigated by the police, properly. I'll make sure of that.'

'Daddy, this is terrible.'

'I am so sorry, Helen.'

'Oh, and where's Cleo? Is she all right?'

David had been looking after my dog Cleo while I was away.

My father had bought her as a present for my eighteenth birthday, after our other dog died. Why on earth am I asking about Cleo when I've just heard my brother has died? Am I mad? What should I say here? I hear my father breathing, trying to control himself.

'Cleo's fine. David took her back to Bill's, before ...' He gulps air and starts explaining, again.

'Helen, it was an accident. Your mother and I had just come back from holiday, but I've told you that already. I'm sorry, I can't think straight. I ought to tell you that there was a gun in the room.'

'A gun? Whose gun was it? What kind of a gun?'

'We don't know, we can't be certain if anyone else was there. The back door wasn't locked, maybe someone got in and there was a tussle. I don't know. That's how I got in, and, I –' his voice catches. 'Found David. On the floor. His head.' My father is struggling. 'There were gunshot wounds.' He pauses, as if to let this sink in.

It sinks. I am sinking down, down.

'We don't know much else at this stage. There wasn't anyone else there when I got there. The house will be closed off whilst the police make their enquiries, including why my client must have left that cabinet open.'

Cabinet? A gun cabinet? I think this, but don't trust myself enough to say anything.

'Someone must have broken in. There were empty bottles, a lamp's been knocked over. I just don't know what happened. It must have been an accident unless it was a fight. David wouldn't have given in without a fight. He is – oh God – was, so strong. I'm co-operating, of course I am, and the coroner will be involved, the police say. He would have to be. They said he might have died a day or so before I found him.'

My father sobs again. Peter squeezes my arm.

My father says, 'Helen this is difficult to tell you, especially with all these miles between us. Your mother can't get to the phone at the moment. She's ... It's been hard on her. I can't really talk about it. Will you come home? We can talk more then? Your mother will need you. I probably shouldn't take up too much time – this call is expensive, though that's not the point. But we need ... Would you?'

I've let him go on for too long without reassuring him that I'll head back across the Atlantic. I thought I had got away. Somewhere inside me a door clangs shut.

'Yes, yes, of course. I'll look into getting a flight. I don't know how I'll do it yet but I'll come. Are you all right, Daddy? Is Mummy? This must be awful for you.'

It was awful for me too, but no one was asking me how I felt.

I promise to sort things out. Goodbyes are exchanged and I turn to Peter and hand him back the telephone receiver. He gives me a quick semi-hug by putting his hands on my shoulders and pushing them slightly together. He doesn't know what to do with me.

'Did you know?' I ask.

'Yes,' Peter responds. 'Your father called me before lunch. I knew your brother had sadly died, but' (he's the second person to tell me, how many others know already?) 'not any details. I'm sorry, Helen. I didn't know what the best thing was – I thought you might want, or at least it would be a good thing, if we went on to have this lunch before you spoke to your father. Everything will be different for you now. I wanted you to have some time first.' He pauses and looks at me. 'How are you?'

He is kind. I don't cry then. I find it is hard to speak. 'I'm, umm, not sure. It hurts. I don't know what to say.'

'Let's go back home, then. Angie can take care of you there. She's a good person.'

Nothing – no one – is going to be able to help.

In the comfort of their Mississippi home I lie on plump sofas, with puffy, squashy cushions and soft, clinging blankets. 'I'm so sorry,' people say. 'This must be a nightmare.' 'Such a terrible loss.' I am told I can talk or I don't need to talk, and I can do – must do – whatever I want to do. I have no clue what I want to do. Wanting to do something seems like such a luxury, a million miles from where I am, trying to get through the next minute.

They ask what happened and I repeat what I can of my father's account. I try to use my newly-fledged lawyer's brain to look at information, not interpretation. Stick to the facts. Emotions are not relevant. That had been hammered into me in my law degree.

Those minimal facts I have are picked over. Do you think he might have taken his own life? they ask me. I shrug. Others nod. I can't say yes. My father thinks something else happened. Or is he hanging onto the possibility that something else happened? It is an act of anger, is suicide, I am told, a way of taking revenge on the person you were angry with. Is there anyone else who might have found David? I mumble, 'I don't know.' The questioning – the fact they are even talking like this – seems very American.

When the tears come, they come from a void of nothing but pain, when I'm alone. This crater now inside me will become very familiar – almost, you could say, like home.

Arrangements are made to change my flight to the earliest available. I tell my parents when I am coming home; in a couple of days. I learn that neither my parents, nor anyone else, will pick me up from Heathrow so I'll need to catch a train to Doncaster.

I am now heading home. The fact. Not the emotion.

I am dropped off at St Louis airport. 'Please don't come in with me, I'll be fine. I don't want any long goodbyes. You've been really kind, but I just want to be on my own now.' I have a bit of persuading to do. Poor things. It can't be easy being around me, anyway. I'm only part human, mostly zombie. I must remember to do things. Get up out of bed, ('get up, get up, you've got to get up!') breathe, go to the loo, put clothes on, eat (not so good at that), brush teeth. Their compassion made me desperate to leave.

The airport feels almost black although my eyes would like to tell me it is bright and my ears want to inform me about announcements of flights, delays, keep an eye on your luggage, that kind of thing, but it's all a blur and my racing brain takes in little. I had arrived at the airport without any cash and was going to have to wait until I got on the flight for anything to eat or drink, which I was cursing myself for.

I remember I need to call Jane, an old school friend I spent a month with in New York, to tell her I won't be returning. I ask the operator to reverse charge the call.

'Hi, it's me. Thanks for accepting the call. Stupid of me, I've run out of cash.' I tell Jane what has happened, practising a version which I'm going to have to say many times.

'I am so sorry Helen, I can't imagine …'

'So, you hadn't heard then?'

'No, this is such a shock. God, it's awful, I never would have expected it. How are you? I only saw him at Christmas, when you and I came back from my aunt's for drinks, you remember?'

She knows my family; her father John is a solicitor in the same town and he also went to Cambridge. I remember last Christmas; it is not something easily forgotten. We talk for a while, in the way that you can to someone you've known for ages.

'I'm heading back to Doncaster now, just wanted to tell you I won't be coming back to New York. Please let's not talk any more about David, I can't. Tell me something, ask me a question, treat me like I'm normal.'

'Things are the same here really, I don't know what to say right now. Oh, OK, one thing, can you please tell me something? How did it go, that lunch with Quentin Crisp? Did you really do it, did it happen? It seems mad asking you now. I'd been wondering.'

Jane knows that I was ambitiously planning a book of interviews with gay icons to fundraise for the fight against AIDS. We both already know too many people who are affected by – have even died of – AIDS. Quentin Crisp was first on my list.

'I did! Far out! His name was actually in the telephone directory, and his number. I took him for lunch at the Algonquin, like a real interview, you know, where Dorothy Parker used to hang out? The waiter looked at his face, blue coiffed hairdo and everything, asked him, "What would Madam like to drink?" dropped his eyes to his trousers and corrected himself, "Sorry. Sir", without missing a beat. What a charmer that man is. He said he lived freely in New York, no getting beaten up there for being gay and out.' I exhale. 'That's a different world now. Don't expect I'll be writing anything now.' I'd tried to keep the pain away and talk about something from my past life but I start to feel sorry for myself again and I can feel tears coming. This isn't working.

'You will, one day. Listen, now's not the time, but when we're both back, when you're properly in London, I'll tell you more about what's been going on in New York. I think it might be just the thing for you,' Jane says, and we say our goodbyes.

I try to settle into reading *Kane and Abel* by Jeffrey Archer, a borrowed book, but it is for show really. I can't even imagine finishing a book again. My watch has broken so I look around to find a clock.

'Do you need the time?' asks a man in a grey cashmere coat. I notice his coat, then his watch, expensive with lots of dials on it. I look up to see an attractive, square-jawed man, a clean white shirt with an open collar above a muscular, thickset body. He has a warm smile. My body instantly responds. Good grief – is nature so bloody determined it now wants to try and make babies? No!

'Ten thirty-two. At least it is here,' he says, smiling at the various dials on his watch. 'Four thirty-two in the afternoon at home. Are you going to Heathrow by any chance?'

We are both waiting at the gate for the same flight. 'Yes.' I almost add, 'Sherlock.' He has a businessman's voice with a Midlands accent. Maybe from Nottingham?

The same pain is still there, but now there is a different feeling. What the hell am I thinking of? I must be going mad.

I turn back to my book. He persists. 'We've got a bit of time to wait for the plane. Would you perhaps like a drink? I wouldn't normally ask young ladies if they'd like a drink but, well, why not?'

'No. thank you.' If I start talking, I shall have to say the thing that happened. I don't know what to say.

'Are you sure? I'm going to have one. It helps me sleep on the flight. Or even if I don't sleep it helps anyway.' He laughs easily. 'It's entirely up to you. I don't mind one way or the other. But I'll feel better about drinking if you join me.'

'Maybe I will, then. I'll have a brandy.' I surprise myself.

'Of course,' he answers smoothly, 'On the rocks?' I nod. He returns with a brandy glass, possibly a triple, and what looked like whisky for him.

'There you go. I've been on a business trip here, in St Louis. Will be glad to get back to the UK. No more travelling for a while. You?'

'I've been on a trip. I came back from Mexico last week.' That seems eons ago. 'I have to go back to London now, and then home, back up North.'

'Will you be glad to be back?'

'No. But I don't have any option.'

Oh God, I start to cry. Snotty crying, too. And no bloody tissues, I'd used them up on the journey to the airport.

'I thought there was something about you. I've got broad shoulders. And,' he produces a handkerchief out of his top pocket with a small flourish, 'this. Here you go, it's yours.'

I hiccup something like 'Thank you.'

'You don't have to tell me anything,' he says. 'We can talk about the weather if you'd like. What's the weather been like in St Louis? Probably worse than Mexico?'

We chat, I don't remember what about.

After a while, he puts a hand on my shoulder, looking directly into my eyes all along, so he can check I'm OK with it. I could say no but I don't. I have no strength to resist. Then when he puts an arm around me, I can't help but snuggle into his shoulder. The cashmere coat feels good; he smells good. He pulls me closer. I sink into the seat, even though it's hard, an airport seat. After a while he kisses the top of my head, quite gently. I drink my brandy and cough at the impact of it. He drinks his whisky a bit slower.

An announcement comes for our (our!) flight to begin boarding.

'Where are you sitting?' he asks.

'Row 45, E.'

'I'm towards the front.' Of course. He had to be. 'But I'm going to come and find you. Don't worry. Let's go board that plane. You'll be OK.' How would he know that?

We move towards the queue. He waits with me, talking about nothing at all and I appreciate the effort.

I walk to the back of the plane while he is seated in business class.

But then he does come to the back. And he finds a seat not far behind mine, where there is a whole empty row by the window.

'Would it be it OK if we move back here, just for a while?' he asks the air hostess. 'My friend here has had a sad loss. You wouldn't mind?' That smile again. She smiles back, agrees, looks at me and brings another blanket. Cashmere man sorts out some more drinks, miniatures. I don't like brandy but I drink it. St Bernard dogs bring brandy to warm up skiers stranded in the snow, don't they?

Cashmere man turns his full attention back to me.

'Now then, mystery girl. You don't have to say anything, of course, but if you want to talk, I can listen. I have a feeling that if you did talk, it might be easier for you. Only tell me what you want to. And remember, you don't have to say a thing.'

I talk. I tell him the story, what I know of it anyway, in between sips of brandy and crying and having tears wiped away. Neither of us sleeps. His arm draws me closer, he kisses me, and when everyone else sleeps, we fumblingly join what I had thought was a glamorous mile high club under a blanket in the sky. It briefly delivers more than the St Bernard's liquid comfort. I drift into light sleep as the aircraft goes dark.

Chapter 4

Summer 1965, Leahurst, Tickhill

'Cross your heart?' my mother says.

'Cross my heart and hope to die!' I say, looking straight at the black centres of her blue eyes, crossing my heart with one hand and crossing the fingers of the other hand behind my back.

'Well then, I will tell you,' says my mother, although I still think she isn't my mother, and this might be when she confesses. 'But you must never, ever tell anyone else.'

I nod, hard as I can. 'I won't. I've crossed my heart, haven't I?'

'You can't always believe what your eyes tell you. Think of Grandpa and his magic. You didn't really think he ate that goldfish at your birthday party, did you?'

Yes, I did, that's why I felt sick too. 'Of course not,' I say.

'Come closer; let me whisper.' She takes my long plait, the one Mervyn pulls every day when he follows me into school even though I hate it, moves it out of the way of my ear, and leans right in so that I can smell her perfume, Chanel No. 5.

'I can make people trip over. I only have to look at them and I can make them trip over. Just like that. Strangers. Anyone. It only takes a moment. I can teach you if you like?'

Is that it? I feel myself growing red.

'Aren't you going to say anything, Helen? Oh, but you're far too sensitive. And you think too much.'

'I can't help it, thinking.' I decide to brave it. 'When I come into a room and there's grown-ups there, they stop talking.'

'Silly girl. That's nothing. And there was me thinking you'd want to know about my special power. But maybe you know all the same. You and me, we're one. I'm inside you like you were once inside me, seven years ago now.'

Her heartbeat drowns out mine; crushes my smallness. I need more air. I look out through the window towards the garden.

'Go on then, run along outside and play. Take David with you. And stop imagining so much, it won't do you any good.'

David is playing with Lego on a blanket on the floor, with Treever next to him. I offer him my open hand and smile; it's hard not to

Monica Garlick, 1962

when you see him. Gold-blond hair, cobalt eyes over a freckly nose, scuffed, skinny knees in big shorts, pockets stuffed with his riches, including a matchbox car, a glint of marbles, a baked conker, a twist of yellow string.

'Gopn ngont to, ngun gogo me.' He smiles back, making his eyes turn into upside down crescent moons, and the kitchen's brightness gets sunnier.

'What's he saying?' asks Mum.

'He says he'd like a milky coffee with two sugars, a boiled egg and soldiers.'

What he actually said was that he didn't want to play outside, he wants to play with Lego. But his Rice Krispies are inside the dog and unless he eats something now, he'll starve.

'Oh, all right then.' She smiles at David, her golden child. 'Don't tell your father, Helen. He'll say I'm too soft on him.'

That's an easy promise. No one wants to tell Daddy things he doesn't like to hear.

David scrambles up onto his light blue stool at the table before playing with his egg and soldiers, one of the things he'll eat. Sometimes sausages and chips. And mashed up banana with sprinkled sugar. Biscuits and sweeties too, but he can't survive on those.

'One day,' I start. He likes a 'One day' story. He looks up before he puts a dippy egg-yolked soldier in his mouth. I see him thinking he'll give the rest to Treever.

'Eat up now, just one more mouthful, here's the aeroplane and you're the hangar and neeeeow, in it pops. There. One day, we'll have a fire under the stars and eat what we want. We'll live like Cowboys and Indians and ride our ponies, free as the wind.'

'Ike on tow?' asks David.

'Yes, like Tonto.'

I fiddle with the soldiers, adding jam to appeal to the hangar. David is taking ages.

'I'm bored,' I say.

'What do you want me to do?' says our mother. 'Go and read a book or play outside. I've got other things to do.'

We have an au pair, Jean, from the village in Cornwall where we go on holiday, to the Salt Box, but it's Jean's day off. Mum has a cleaner, Mrs Porter, and a gardener, her husband Mr Porter, who'd had to stop going down the coal mine because of his lungs. Mum doesn't feed or walk the dog, that's my job. She's decorating the house with tapestries she rescued from being thrown away, filling the house with furniture from auctions, including a gigantic dining table which she bought for £16, painting colours everywhere.

Cooking is her main thing, vying with reading, she says. Mum taught me to read when I was three. Reading is my favourite thing. I told her when I was little, after she'd asked me, that I wanted to be a writer when I grew up, but she said I couldn't because writers don't make any money so I needed to be a solicitor like Daddy first. I heard Daddy on the phone saying that his son was going to be a solicitor but it didn't matter what his daughter did because she was a girl. So now I think it might actually be a good thing if I'm a solicitor.

Anyway, today I have to look after my brother.

'Do you need the loo yet, David?' I ask, dreading waiting the age until he's 'been'.

David ignores me, jumps down and starts to run out of the door, until he catches my mother's eye, slowing to a walk till he's out of sight, speeding up over the garden lawn. I follow as fast as I can get away with. 'Don't run!' my mother warns.

The sun glowing through the yew hedge draws us into the garden, then on to jump over the shafts of sun piercing the apple trees in the orchard. Our golden retriever follows. Everyone laughed when David called the dog 'Treever', and it stuck. He was bought because dogs terrified me after an Alsatian bit me in a snicket when I was walking to school. My father had the idea to get a puppy, though my mother said she wouldn't look after it unless she really had to, which would be never. When we saw the puppies, balls of golden candy floss, a waggy-tailed girl came over to us and was nice and licked us, but my parents said we should choose the best of the litter, which was, the breeder said, this one. Later, my father said we should have got the girl. But Treever is a good guard dog and looks after us.

Our house, Leahurst, is a long, red brick rectangle of an old rectory set sideways onto Sunderland Street, a busy street joining Yorkshire to Nottinghamshire. A high wall shelters a magic willow tree, good for hiding under to read, and a bright central burst of peonies, with lupins, delphiniums, snapdragons, drifts of lily of the valley and forget-me-nots by the walls. A yew hedge protects raspberry, strawberry and gooseberry beds. One wall backs on to a cricket ground beyond. On the left of our walled garden is an apple orchard

Leahurst, Tickhill

with a tumbledown shed, and beyond that an arched doorway leading to a little pony paddock, with a hawthorn hedge running right around it, and allotments on the left. The paddock has a three-sided, brick-built stable with a pointy roof, missing a few bricks and tiles on the top right side, but enough to shelter a pony from the rain. It is also still missing a pony.

I've been wishing hard to fix that. While grey is the proper horsey name for white if you know about horses, my dream pony – which could even be an actual unicorn or Pegasus – is the white of a dove's feather. I not only dream about white ponies, I play at ponies, jump over an upturned mop and bucket in the garden, and talk about them almost all the time.

Taking my campaign a stage further, I wrote a letter to Robert Robinson on *Junior Points of View*. 'It's in the post,' I told my mum. 'It's not fair that you won't let me have a pony. I've even saved up nineteen shillings and sixpence. It would have been nineteen shillings and ten pence but I paid for the stamp.'

'Don't be ridiculous. Robert Robinson will never read it out. He gets hundreds of letters every day, probably thousands. Come down a peg or two and go and have your bath.'

The next morning at school, my classmates crowded round. I was famous.

'They read out your letter, Helen Garlick. Your letter said there weren't enough horse and pony programmes on telly. They showed a programme about horses.'

'Did they? My mum sent me to have a bath. She said it would never happen.'

'They did. They showed your letter. On the telly! You said you've saved up nineteen shillings and sixpence to help buy a pony.' They had me there.

'You're rich, Helen Dalek! Won't you buy us sweeties after school from Snell's?'

'I can't. I'm saving it up for a pony, like it said in the letter.'

'Oh, go on. Just a sherbet fountain. Please?'

'No.'

'It's not fair! Helen Garlick's a Dalek, Helen Garlick's a Dalek. Exterminate! Exterminate!' said Mervyn, before pulling my plait again. 'You're horrible, Helen Dalek.'

They walked off, before I even had chance to say, 'Sticks and stones can break my bones but calling names won't hurt me,' like my mum had told me to try. When you're the one in class always with your hand up to answer a question, and you love reading and often have your head inside a book, there are reasons why other kids might not like you.

That evening, I dared to state, 'You were wrong, Mummy. Robert Robinson did read out my letter on the telly. Everybody knows now that I want a pony.'

'Race you t' gate. 'Arn't 'atch me!' yells David as his skinny legs pelt into the orchard. 'Yes I can! I'm coming to get you.' I hold my breath, counting to three to give him a head start, then run as fast as I can, gaining ground over the time it takes to get to the paddock gate. Looking behind to see how close I am, David trips over a dead apple branch and bang, hits his head on the ground. I'm right behind him and we fall in a heap. 'Ooow,' croons David, rubbing his head, biting his bottom lip. My elbow hurts: my funny bone took the fall, though I don't know why anyone calls it that.

'What's that, David?' I ask, pointing behind him, this time not only to distract him. David turns around to look at the trembling, browny-grey creature with swollen red eyes, lids barely open, pus blocking up its nose, ears drooping down to the gravel path. It's by the nets that protect the raspberry canes.

'A bunny,' whispers David. 'It's not really well. Is it dead?'

'No, it can't be.' I watch and listen. 'Is it shivering?'

'Poor bunny. What's to do?'

'We can try to save it. But we might have to put it out of its misery.'

I copied that from what our mother said to Mrs Pickles from next door when she ran over a cat in her car and no one expected it to live. Maybe it meant we'd have to telephone the vet. Maybe it would have to go to sleep for ever.

'We'll save it, us,' says David, pointing at me then himself. I nod and start to make a list. My mother makes lists, sometimes several times a day.

'One. What do they eat?' I whisper to David. It will be good for him to work this out.

'Pete' Rabbi' eats 'rrots from Mr M'Gregor's gar'n and has 'momile tea when he's been a naughty boy.' That's a long speech for him. He grins.

'We'll need a box and a blanket.' I count on my fingers, two and three. 'Back to one. Food. I'm not sure about the carrots or lettuce, we might get into trouble. But we can get grass. And water.'

'I'll get my toy bo',' says David, 'And water.'

'I'll pick nice bits of grass, and there's that blanket Treever's got outside.'

David gets up, wincing at the throbbing bump on his head. He hates showing he's hurt, even aged five. He walks slower to the back door to go into the kitchen.

'Don't worry, we'll look after you.' I turned back to the rabbit. 'You'll get better, once you've had a nice lie down.'

I hear my mother calling from the kitchen. 'Helen!'

I don't want to go back inside. Maybe it will die if I leave it on its own. Stretching out my hand, I give it a pat on its back, the first time I've ever touched a rabbit. It's hot, hotter than Treever, but so soft. It flinches, but doesn't run away. I'll have to wash my hands now. Heaven knows what germs I'll have picked up, as Grannie would say.

'I'm coming,' I call back.

Fast-walking back to the kitchen, I see David there, holding on with one hand to our mother's skirt: white and red polka dots, cinched in tight with a black patent belt. His fair head is craned back to look at her, a reluctant tear streaking his cheek, his other hand pushing away the gold and red biscuit tin.

The sun from the window lights up the red gold corn of my mother's hair to make it gleam fire. Her hair, reflecting the shade of my brother's, is swept up, flattened into a sleek coil, which tames her frizzy curls. Perhaps she's going out tonight? Her hair looks like that when she's meeting friends. Though that seems to make our father cross and so he closes the drawing room door and conducts his classical music on the gramophone, even when he is supposed to be looking after us.

I tense a little, seeing the look on my mother's face.

'I told you not to run, now see.' Her lips are tight. 'You're the eldest. You're the responsible one and you should know better.' But David wasn't crying because of the head bump.

'Mee 'ant a bo', a bo', a BO', 'leeaase, mummmeee,' repeats David, looking at her, brushing away the tear and wiping his hand on her skirt. My mother studies the mark on her skirt in distaste, then turns to me.

'You said you want a biscuit, David, and it's custard creams, your favourites, but that's not apparently what you want today.' I like biscuits. Mummy usually says I can't have any more than three but we're lucky if we get two down David. My mother snaps the tin lid shut and put it back on the highest cupboard shelf.

'I can get "please" and "Mummy" but nothing else,' she says, turning to me. 'Why can't he talk properly? He'll be starting school soon.'

There's no time for this. 'There's a poorly rabbit in the orchard, we want to save it and we need a cardboard box.' David looks at me and nods his head.

'You can't bring it in here,' sighs my mother. 'I don't want any more animals in the house. Especially not poorly ones. I don't do animals, you know that.'

We already have Jackson the budgerigar who was given to us and a goldfish I'd won at a fair, called Timothy because that's my favourite name. We're pushing it.

'I know, Mummy. We're going to put it in ...' I look over at David for a clue.

'Innn op it al. Neemal op it al!' squeals David, 'In nnner sss 'ed.' He hops from one foot to the other, delighted. We're in this together, as we usually are.

'In our own animal hospital, you know, in the shed, like he says, in the orchard. You don't need that old shed, it's a waste.' I'm warming up now, ending with what might tip the balance. 'And we'll be out of the way. You won't notice we're there.'

'You'll have to ask your father when he comes back from the office.'

'OK. I promise,' I call out, heading to the staircase, pulling David's hand to go up to his bedroom and find his box, one stair at a time, being careful.

The toybox has his Andy Pandy in it, with a round startled face, fair hair curling out under a tricorn hat, blue and white stripes on a bendy body and bright white shoes that you could never wear in the country, an Incredible Hulk, a tin spinning top, his matchbox cars, a ball, a wooden sword, and who knows what. He grabs the box and up-ends it. Andy Pandy is flung any old where, and we bolt back down the stairs through the red and blue stained-glass door to find out if the rabbit is still there, grabbing the blanket and a plant pot saucer for its water on the way.

The rabbit hasn't moved but it hasn't died either. David moves in closer. His little, practical hands reach under its body, placing it gently to lie in the box before he carries it over to the shed. David is often braver than me. I'm sturdier in looks but he can watch the Daleks sitting on the sofa. I need to be behind it.

I make a sign on a torn-off piece of cardboard box with a blue Bic biro, drawing the edges of the capital letters, then scribbling in the blank middles.

ANIMAL HOSPITAL. NO ADULTS.

I pin it on the door with gold drawing pins, before asking my father. He'll say yes. He likes animals.

•

David and I played for hours that summer in the brick shed with the dead ivy fronds trailing through the cracks in its roof. We rescued a broken-winged blackbird, other rabbits with myxomatosis, baby birds that had fallen out of nests, a half-chewed mouse or two we'd saved from Sir John Barbirolli (or Puss-Puss for short), the cat who always lived outside and was nearly always sneezing. Even a stag beetle, which reared up on its back legs and waved its front legs around.

I thought then that I could make everything better if I tried hard enough. But, as my mother explained to me, 'Helen, you need to know that the animals will all die. Don't hope too much, it's for the best.'

Everything did die in the animal hospital, usually overnight, sometimes a few days later. Maybe using the dog's blanket was not the cleverest thing to have done.

Chapter 5

4th March 1981

'How are you getting back?' cashmere man asks, getting ready to go back to his seat just before the flight starts its descent.

'I'll get the underground back to London and then a train to Doncaster.'

'I'm not going to let you do that. I'll take a taxi with you to King's Cross. You can go on from there. But you're going to have to let me help you before that. No question.'

He moves forward to business class while I go to the loo and clean up with tissues and toothpaste in the tiny space. I catch sight of myself in the mirror, shame biting, along with the after-effects of brandy. I am startled to see how much I look like my mother.

We disembark, collect our luggage. I get into a taxi with him and we arrive at King's Cross. On the way I learn he is married.

'But we're going to see each other again,' he says. I say, 'Never.' It is an absolute rule of mine never to go out with a married man.

'I want to know that you're going to be all right. I need to see you,' he says.

'I'll be all right. Even if I'm not, that's none of your business. Go to your wife and love her. But,' (manners!) 'um, thank you.' I brush him off, mortified. I must go back to my parents. I walk towards the train, looking back once, when I think he might have stopped looking, to catch his face before it gets too small. He still is looking.

I sleep on the train and dream of snakes and a well and churned-up earth. Maybe if I knew what it meant it might explain why, although I'm desperate with grief at losing my brother, I have just had it off with a married man. I have no compass. I am falling.

I wake up around Peterborough, with the sing-song tone of the announcer. Will both my parents come or just my father? Maybe she'll have another migraine. I haven't yet spoken to my mother, since … She loves – correction, loved – David so much. I must put things in the past tense now, practise what to say now everything has changed. But it still will be 'loves'. She won't stop because he is dead. I dread seeing my mother.

The train is not busy. As it slowly pulls into Doncaster station, the sky is leaden, the platform's brown paving stones rain-wet. My parents are on the platform to meet me: a first. My father stands with his left hand half held up, as if he's trying to work out whether he should raise it in greeting. Mum is behind, camel coated, a green scarf masking her neck against the cold, her eyes on the ground. With an effort she looks up to see where I am, trying a smile. They look smaller. No one is ever going to be able to fix this family, fix me, now. I am home.

Chapter 6

Summer 1968

This life in Tickhill, our relative idyll, lasted a few years. David grew like a bean-pole, athletic too, taking his stabilisers off before me, although I had to then because it was embarrassing, me being older and everything. We played together lots and spent hours outside. As well as playing football and cricket, David was learning to look at the stars and collect birds' eggs and go fishing. We both went pony-riding.

I was sent for ballet lessons and elocution classes in Donny, where we learned to recite, for example:

> *My father's car is a Jaguar*
> *He drives it rather fast*
> *Castles farms and draughty barns*
> *We go charging past*
> *Arthur's cart is far less smart*
> *And can't go half as fast*
> *But I'd rather ride in Arthur's cart*
> *Than my Papa's fast car.*

With a long 'aar' rather than the whipcrack of the Yorkshire 'a'. I was even learning to play the piano like my mother, starting with my right hand. The *Moonlight Sonata* was her favourite: the sound of her playing drifting through the drawing room window was dreamy. We stayed with our grandparents regularly, most weekends, and went to Cornwall in summer, or if we were home our parents would sometimes take us out for a day in Filey or Bridlington for candy-floss and fish and chips. The sun mostly shone and, as far as I can remember, this lasted until I was nearly ten and David eight.

My father went out to work at his own firm of solicitors in Waterdale, Doncaster: G C Garlick & Co. He usually came home for dinner at 6.30 p.m. One day, he came home an hour earlier.

'David, Helen, I want to talk to you about something, so hurry up, it's important,' he said. He could see that David was surreptitiously feeding the dog under the table. I saw my father's flash of irritation, as my mother looked into the distance.

'Come on David, you just finish off, and I'll clear,' I said. My father was probably more interested in his announcement than another battle with David about food.

'We're ready now,' I said, finishing clattering plates.

'Right. Well, I have been to an auction. Do you know what an auction is?'

'Yes! Sometimes ponies are sold at auctions, aren't they Daddy?' I gave him a big smile. This sounded promising.

I was still hoping for my dream white pony. I was, in truth, obsessed. My father, prompted by everyone knowing I wanted a pony, acquired an old pit pony when the coal mines closed, having seen the attractive word 'free' right next to 'pony' in an ad. Box (the pony) was bay, namely brown and black and, apart from being a pony, he had nothing in common with my dream. I still knew I should be grateful and had to say 'Thank you,' to Daddy and look like I properly meant it. At twenty-five years old and never ridden before, Box was what we learned to call a character. He liked grass, and developed a number of other likes now that his life was overground – specifically, people and cricket. When a cricket match was on in summer, Box would walk through the hedge, his coal-coarsened skin undeterred by its thorns, to watch. He would also sometimes get out and stand by the bus stop. Mum would be alerted to this by the postlady, who kept her eye on things, including Box. 'Missus Garlick, yer'd better get out 'ere, your Box is trying to catch t'bus to Doncaster. 'Ee won't move from t'queue. Be quick.' And my mother would run out to get the halter, catch Box, and bring him back to his paddock with its unreliable boundary.

'Well, maybe. But this is nothing to do with ponies. Something much better than that, which will make us all happy.'

Hiding my disappointment, I glanced at my mother. I thought I saw what might have been a tear in her eye.

'You will remember this day in future because it will change all of our lives. I have bought a house at an auction,' continued my father. 'It's very grand, built in 1689, when William and Mary were on the throne. Eight bedrooms, three bathrooms and a cloakroom, a big garden, an orchard and paddock. With real oil paintings on the walls. I've the particulars right here. We'll all be proud to live there.'

With a flourish, he placed down on the table a black and white brochure with a big, grey house like an empty doll's house, perfectly symmetrical, chilling as a horror movie still. There was a red table-cloth on the family table. Things in Leahurst, our home, had colour. The brochure stuck out, as if it knew it didn't fit.

'But that doesn't mean we'll have to move there, does it? I don't want to. All my friends are here. Treever's here. And Box. Everything is here.'

'We don't want to move,' David said and he burst into tears. My mother couldn't stop herself from weeping then. A sunny boy, even when my father whacked him – which he did, sometimes unpredict-ably – David rarely cried. It was his badge of honour. And I only saw

Mum cry once, when she had the night-bleed in bed which meant that my baby sister wouldn't be born.

My father's face flushed. 'I make the decisions round here. Do I need to tell you that? We're moving to Slade Hooton Hall and that's an end to it. Go upstairs to your room. And don't come down till you know how to behave.'

I abandoned them for my bedroom, hurling myself upstairs and banging through the door to hide in my walk-in cupboard. David came up behind me. I heard him open the bedroom door and hesitatingly step in. From the cupboard, I said, 'It's all right David. I'm here.' One lie, one truth. When he hid in the cupboard too, I clung to him, even though by this time he didn't often let me hold him in my arms. Our world was shattering. Daddy was right, this would change our lives. But I could already sense a dreadful feeling that while there was nothing I could do to stop it, this decision would be the worst thing that had ever happened to us.

Chapter 7

4th March 1981, Doncaster

My father opens the door of the train carriage and helps me down with my cases as I step slowly onto the platform. I know I should hug them.

My mother speaks. 'Darling, thank you for coming back home.'

'That's OK, Mum. I'm sorry it's taken me all this time. I'm so sorry. This is so awful.' I didn't intend to cry.

My mother looks at the ground again, then looks at me and I search her face. Her eyes are flattened, their blue a washed-out grey, her pupils tiny pinpoints, her blond hair whiter.

I can't not wrap my arms around my mother's camel-coated, hunched figure. Her heavy body heaves inside the hug without a sound. I break away, turn to face my father and swerve my face to the side as he tries to kiss me near my lips. My Nana, his mother, used to do that too. He has a crusty cold sore on the right edge of his mouth. I wipe off my left cheek with my right hand when he looks in the opposite direction.

My dad explains he has parked the Daimler a little further along from the station.

'We got here early,' he says, almost apologetically. 'It wasn't raining then.'

We slowly walk towards the car.

'How was your journey?'

'OK.'

'It's been raining quite a bit over the last few days. I thought there might be a bit of sun today but the sun hasn't got his hat on.' He tries to smile.

My mother shoots him a look, a watered-down version. He looks down, saying nothing. I cannot find any words to offer up as a balm.

'Peter sends his best.' I try to find a tissue in my coat pocket as the tears are falling again, but instead find cashmere man's handkerchief, smelling of his aftershave.

We walk up the three hundred or so yards to the Daimler. It is parked sideways, crossing over two spaces, and there's a man waiting nearby to park his car. He winds his window down.

'Gerrout of it, why can't yer bloody park straight?' he shouts. We look at him.

'My brother's dead,' I say to the man. He turns his head away and revs the accelerator a bit but he doesn't say anything else.

'Would you like to go in the front?' my mother asks. I get carsick in the back.

'Are you sure, Mum?' She shrugs and tries to smile. 'No, don't worry, you go in the front. I'll go in the back.'

My father pulls his car out and round along Waterdale, where his offices sit on the first and second floor above Lloyds Bank, opposite the Victorian St James' Baths where we learned to swim. Every time he passes his office, my father will look up to check everything is OK, but this time he doesn't. He stares glassily, leaning towards the window in his driving seat, from time to time moving his hand up over his head, dragging strands of hair over the top as he drives, often checking in the mirror.

I look up and see the familiar gold lettering bordered by black, 'G C Garlick & Co.', and recall how my dad used to say to David, as he spat on his handkerchief, with David trying to wriggle away as the smell of spit lingered worse than the smudge of smut, 'And one day it will say G C Garlick & Son.' He stopped saying that when David had to leave his second polytechnic for failing his exams. Then he started saying things like, 'And when you take over the firm, Helen, it will say G C Garlick & Daughter.' It didn't seem to matter how many times I told him that was never going to happen.

We also pass the white and black Doncaster Arts Centre on the right, where my parents helped to found the Doncaster Film Society, and on the left just by the traffic lights on the crossroads stands the Gaumont (now a cinema), where my mum once saw the Beatles perform.

When we get to 13 Albion Place, the tall black and white Georgian terraced house my parents moved into after they sold Slade Hooton Hall, there is no place to park at the front on the busy road. My father has to drive further along, nearer the newsagents, so there's a slightly longer walk. My mother sighs as I pull out my cases from the boot.

As we pass the shop, the owner inside calls out to my father, 'Hello there Geoffrey, how are you? And is it your daughter home now?'

My father nods, walking on.

'He doesn't know?' I ask.

He shakes his head. 'As you can see, no. I'll tell him tomorrow, when I get the paper, I've just been choosing my time. Everyone round here will know soon enough.'

We arrive at the front door, and my father opens it. As if no one else is there, he talks to himself. I think he says, 'That bobbin.'

Out of the corner of my eye, I glimpse a net curtain twitching behind the bay window on the ground floor of the house next door. When I look, the net curtain is stilled, but no longer properly shields its window.

'How many people have you told?' I ask.

'The family of course, and the office staff, and Granville and Gwen and the Laughton vicar. And Jem, you know, the vicar, he's been very good.' He says, 'Your mother hasn't told anyone much yet. Judy and your grandmother have offered to come over to sit with her, to take the pressure off you. I've been making calls. Occasionally people phone us, if they've heard anything. We don't have to answer every call.'

'I can share that with you, if it helps. I can phone people.'

'Not now, Helen. Let's not talk about it. You must be tired, with the journey … I have to go over to Bothamsall Hall tomorrow,' he continues. 'To pick up some of David's things if they'll let me, and see the police officers too. They've got to investigate properly.' His face pinches up into a ball, eyes disappearing, tears squeezing out with sobs.

I judge him so harshly I think I should keep clear of scissors in case I try to cut him.

I look over at my mother. She shrinks further down into her coat.

'I'll come with you, Dad. Maybe I can pick up my car then?'

'Not yet, you can't, the police have still got to do some tests on it or something. They haven't released the car back to us.'

'But it's my car,' I protest, sounding pathetic even to me. I should be nobler.

'It shouldn't take too long. By the way, I said to the police that the Renault was David's car. I mean it was whilst you were travelling. Just in case the police say anything to you. But let's not talk about it now. Let's try and settle down a bit.'

'What about Cleo, when can I collect her?'

'Not yet, Helen, consider your mother.' There is a silence.

'I'll make us a sandwich,' Mum says. 'Cheese? And we've got Branston pickle. Or pickled walnuts,' she suggests. 'Does anyone want any tea? He's bought Dundee cake.'

No one likes Dundee cake much except my father. My mother normally cooks a hot meal in the evenings. We call this meal dinner rather than tea and we eat later than most other people in Doncaster, after the before-dinner drinking is over.

'What would you like to drink?' my father asks me, ignoring her.

'It's a bit early, Dad,' I say. A red flush jumps into his cheeks.

'Well, OK then. What are you having?'

'A gin and tonic, but there's sherry, or wine, or brandy if you'd like. How about a good stiff brandy? There's Courvoisier. You'd like that. Anything you want, Helen.'

I now hate brandy.

'I'll join you.' It is about half past three. There are hours before it will be time to slip away to the relative safety of my still-unfamiliar bedroom. I've only lived in it a few days here and there since I left for Bristol University to read law and they sold Slade Hooton Hall, our teenage home, the year after. My parents use it as the spare room, to store stuff.

He goes over to the drinks cabinet, as well stocked as a chemist's shelf. He unscrews the tonic bottle, pouring it in to a petrol station crystal glass, adding a pre-cut slice of lemon. He sloshes the gin in last, two fingers at least, to hit the drinker first, and then adds more.

I go out to the kitchen to get some ice cubes for the ice bucket, using its tarnished tongs. My mother follows, keeping her eyes on me. She hasn't taken her coat off. I open the fridge door to reach up for the ice tray. The fridge is nearly empty. Bottles of white wine, butter half-wrapped in torn paper, some stilton, rather more crust than anything, old milk, one curled slice of corned beef. The stale smell hits me before I can hold my breath.

The ice tray is a quarter full. I twist it. The cubes don't move so I bang it on the work top. My mother flinches.

'What would you like, Mum?'

'I'll have some tea. I'll do it,' she says. I wait with her.

'Do you want me to go shopping? I could get us some food in for tomorrow,' I say.

'No, it's all right. I'll go to the fish market in the morning. I've got to get out sometime.'

We file back towards the sitting room. My father's glass has been emptied: he is refilling it as we go in.

'I started without you; you don't mind, do you? Here you go, here's yours. Help yourself to ice. Well, it's good that you're home, Helen.' He lifts his glass up and drinks. He'd normally say 'Cheers!' at this point. I'm relieved he doesn't today.

He leans towards me, alcohol on his breath. 'She's not drinking. She went to the doctor yesterday, got something to help, she's not to drink for six months,' Dad whispers.

My mother is sunk in her own world. I focus instead on the one thing that might help. Ignoring the bitter perfumed taste, trying to keep the ice cubes inside the glass, I pour as much down my throat as quickly as I can to reach the click.

My father goes over to the gramophone to choose from his 78 rpm vinyl classical record collection. Sibelius' *Finlandia*. He turns up the volume, then opens out his creased *Daily Telegraph*, to settle into the black plastic sofa with its false fur cushions. He will knock back the G and Ts, then the bargain of the week red wine with the slab of blue and white cheese sandwich with Branston, followed by whisky.

It seems that every time he sits down, the phone rings again. Occasionally I go to answer it, but my father usually motions me away. One time I pick up the receiver myself and dial 123 to listen and talk to the speaking clock, just to give us a bit of peace, but then remember that my dad checks the phone bill and he will notice. Assiduous about calls and letters, he is now concentrating on his story being the one that people hear. I listen to him say 'accident' frequently. Perhaps if he says it often enough, other people will believe it.

My mother gets up out of her chair to go to her bedroom at 8 p.m. Claiming jet lag, I head up to bed too, after kissing them on the cheek, holding my breath, eyes closed.

On the bed on my back, surrounded by unpacked boxes, clothes which aren't mine alongside my cases, I stare at the ceiling. Later, in the depths of a Doncaster darkness I hear my mother's cries, keening like a wounded animal. Nobody mentions it in the morning.

Chapter 8

1973, Slade Hooton Hall

My mother drives the Daimler back from Sheffield with David and me in the rear seat, home to Slade Hooton. My father is in the front. It's Thursday, when he and my mother work together. Mum works now as his secretary in the Sheffield outpost of G C Garlick & Co., an office he recently opened in the city centre, after she declared that she needed to find herself again and work outside the home.

My school report is inside my bag, the brown envelope sealed. I sneak a look, tempted to open it and be done with it, but it will be worse if I do. David's school report is in his bag too, but he has perfected the art of looking as if he doesn't care. I don't know why Mum is driving Dad's car, normally she drives her Triumph Herald. Maybe it has broken down and they can't afford the repairs? As usual, the trip back from school is conducted in near silence, apart from Radio 4.

But the sounds outside are strong, vibrant, steely. Our route is through Tinsley, past the open doors of the steel mills, black and red, hot enough to feel the blast through the car window. Sometimes we see the volcanic molten steel, sparks flying, pouring down into stone troughs to cool. The steel workers' faces are set in concentration: one slip and they could be burned alive. My mother takes the M1 south, then the M18 towards what we now call home. We move from the city, through the big motorways to take the slip road, then down on Cumwell Lane (named after Oliver Cromwell) past the ruins of

Roche Abbey, through the ghostly village of Carr (you hardly ever see anyone there) to mount the high windy ridge towards Slade Hooton, past wide fields, stripped now of hedgerows.

The stolen hedges have been ripped out to maximise wheat planting, and thus profit, by local farmers, including the Smiths, the moon-faced sisters who live up the road in the village. There were once wide grass verges either side of the road, along which, when we first moved here, you could race ponies three abreast. The verges, narrowed by greedy ploughing every year, are now only wide enough for two people to walk side by side. Wildlife suffered too. Now you hear fewer birds singing in Slade Hooton.

I often think about the Smith sisters on this journey. I still bear them a grudge as their farm workers killed Dusty, our cat. Or nearly killed her. Every year, at least once a quarter, their farm workers are armed with shotguns to kill the rats who infest the barns. These barns house giant circular bales of straw next to the silos of harvested grain, and the workers shoot anything that moves. Our Dusty, a slight, beautiful, grey and ginger cat with only half a tail – named after Dusty

Slade Hooton Hall

Springfield, my mother's favourite singer – lived outdoors and usually sheltered in our barn, but fatefully had gone next door to the Smiths' barns on rat-shooting day. She was shot twice, somehow survived, and crawled back under the gate into our barn overnight. I never saw her, what was left, but my brother went searching in the morning, before I was up. He finished her off with a spade to put her out of her misery.

David would only have done that if he absolutely had to; I trusted him. That either of my parents would take responsibility for the death of our cat would not have occurred to us. My mother did not 'do' animals, as she said, often, in case we started imagining anything different. My father was squeamish, not very practical, and would not have taken any sensible action. It was down to David or me, or possibly the gardener, but David didn't want to let Dusty suffer another hour or so before the gardener started work. Nor did he want me to have to do it. But he couldn't hide the pain from me. I don't think anyone else noticed. And he wouldn't talk about it. 'It had to be done,' he said. 'It was quick, at least, well, as quick as I could,' he shrugged and grimaced. I made a sympathetic face, to thank him.

We draw up at the rear, what my mother ironically calls the tradesmen's entrance of Slade Hooton Hall, not going through the white-painted wood and black iron gates to its bleakly imposing front. Those gates are only opened when there are guests staying or coming for dinner. I still can't call it home. Treever is caged in his kennel and run at the back of the barn and barks a few times to say hi. 'I'll walk him,' I say. It will give me a few minutes more, on my own. My father goes inside first, heading for the drawing room with its drinks cabinet. My mother's dark wood Bechstein grand piano is there, brought along from Tickhill, but she rarely plays. I don't play anymore. We hadn't managed to find a piano teacher who would come out to the village so I never progressed beyond playing with my right hand.

My father doesn't seem to feel the cold so much. He puts his chosen classical record on the gramophone and pours himself a stiff gin and tonic, then settles down to read the paper and conduct. We aim not to disturb him.

My mother, camel coat still buttoned up, goes into the kitchen to cook dinner. She turns on all four gas rings on the stove and the grill to warm up the kitchen, then goes down to the cellar to turn on the central heating. We are only allowed by my father to have the heating on once we get back from school, for a maximum of three hours in the evening. It barely makes a dent in the chill. On winter mornings, ice frosts the inside of the upstairs windows. I get dressed for school by bringing my uniform under the sheets, then taking off my pyjamas and dressing myself while still in bed. I promise myself that when I grow up, I will never be this cold again.

I go upstairs to the top floor to change before taking Treever out, passing David's bedroom on the way. The top floor is the stage setting for our nightly terrors, as the ghosts erratically patrol the corridor and go into the billiard room opposite mine. Neither he nor I have seen anything, but their voices and footsteps keep us awake in the night. Three times now, friends of my brothers have stayed in the smaller guest bedroom (posh, us) and each saw the disembodied head of a male ghost wearing a cloth cap staring at them. None of these friends was prewarned. Each one understandably refuses to come back and stay again.

David always wants to leave the light on upstairs at night and sometimes he comes in to snuggle into bed next to me, then we both lie awake, under the blankets, listening to the noises. Neither of us speaks about it to anyone outside, it's too weird. Even inside the house it's not a discussed topic. The only time I dared say anything was to Mum.

'This place is definitely haunted, Mum.'

'Well, if it is, it's benign. It's friendly.'

She kept that line up, even after the 'benign spirit' tried to pull the bedclothes off her bed one night and she and the spirit were in a not-game of tug of war for the relative warmth of her counterpane.

On Friday nights my parents hold big parties at the Hall, mostly for clients, but two of my parents' closest friends always come as they are 'good company'. They are Granville, a gay teacher from Doncaster who teaches the arts to miners' sons and takes them to Stratford every year to experience the theatre, and Evelyn, an accountant originally from Leeds, one of the many places my father professes to dislike. His ever-lengthening list of dislikes includes teachers, especially drama teachers; anyone from Wales, the North West (wrong side of the Pennines) or Birmingham; caravans, roast lamb, short hair on women, long hair on men, Methodists, *Guardian* readers and bossy women. The two latter dislikes he occasionally yells at me as insults. They become beliefs about myself, my rebel badges of honour, defining me. He's also told other people, reported back to me by Aunty Judy and Grannie, that if I ever have a son, he will turn out to be gay. That's too weird; I don't let myself think about it. How Granville and Evelyn don't come under fire I will never understand.

For these parties, my mother puts on grand displays of melon balls with ginger, poached salmon, potatoes dauphinoise, buttered broad beans, beef Wellington, savarin with black cherries and a cheese board with grapes from the vines in our greenhouse (best pretend they are not too sour). She has learned to cook on a cordon bleu course and tosses out helpful titbits. 'Always choose the freshest and best ingredients.' 'Presentation is all.' 'Make sure there is something red in every meal.' There are quantities of French and Spanish wine. Afterwards they play on their Ouija board, the glass circling, careering around, spelling out answers to guests' questions. One guest, a bank manager's wife, ran out of the house too petrified to speak after she'd been given a Ouija board answer. She, too, refuses to come back inside the Hall again.

David and I don't have that option. One day we sneak the Ouija board out and try to set fire to it on a garden bonfire. The damned thing refuses to burn; we have to bury it. Oddly, my parents never mention it again.

This day, my brother and I go into the sitting room next door to put on the gas fire and huddle around it for a while. David will, once he has warmed up a bit, go out into the shed to tinker with his bikes (later motorbikes), which he endlessly takes to pieces and puts back together. He doesn't seem to feel the cold so much either. I am escaping to Sheffield whenever I can now, hormones calling.

•

'I haven't got time to take you. You'll have to walk to the bus if you want to go into Sheffield again. And anyway, why would you want to?' Mum would ask.

I thought the answer was bleeding obvious. Why would I not want to? Choice: cold, bleak, draughty, ghost-ridden house, my only comfort being the dog now my main companion was more into fishing, star-gazing, bikes and Sheffield Wednesday, versus lights, pubs, music, friends, chat, laughter, the promise of sex and drugs (although the latter I avoided, sticking to booze instead. I already suspected I had an addictive personality and I didn't want to take that extra risk. Alcohol seemed safer. Ha!).

Slade Hooton had no local public transport; the nearest bus to Sheffield was at Laughton-en-le-Morthen, just over a mile away. The lure of Sheffield would tug me down the hill from Slade Hooton, an easy route on a small, hedged country road for the first half, down to the little bridge with the stream running under it. The next half was not so easy, the climb up to Laughton, panting to the top and then having to run the last bit. I was so often nearly late, but the buses only ran once an hour at best so it was stupid to miss it.

And then that year there was Meatwhistle too. Meatwhistle crazily stomped into our lives with a big, beautiful plan of putting on *Marat/Sade* as a youth production at the Crucible in Sheffield, itself just opening, during the summer of 1973. In 1964 Peter Brook's production had shocked London. It took another decade to reach the North: fast going.

Meatwhistle, an arts and theatre project, initially got a six-week grant from a far-sighted Sheffield City Council to keep teenagers off the streets – we even had our own building in the city centre's heart. The Holly Building was a permissive, unstructured, creative space where we could do anything, anytime. Up to fifty of us all told, we made music and candles, ate food, danced, talked, acted. It opened doors to our imagination and self-belief. The anarchic energy which emerged spawned the electronic musical careers of The Human League, Heaven 17 (after a wacky start with Musical Vomit, a proto Punk combo who came into being to mock prog rock and play loud two-chord songs with titles like 'I was a Teenage Necrophiliac'), actors, artists, academics and a whole bang load of can-do attitude.

Meatwhistle attracted a diverse teenage group, although the lads took more of the centre stage. My big moment was being cast as Looby Lou in a 'Randy Andy Pandy' sketch with a single Mae West line, 'Is that a gun in your pocket or are you just pleased to see me?'

Glenn Gregory, a willowy blond with flared jeans and a cheese-cloth shirt, came from one of Sheffield's toughest council estates. After he joined, he got regular kickings in the school lunch break. Glenn went on to be an eighties heartthrob in Heaven 17 and later did a world tour singing David Bowie's early back catalogue with the star's blessing in a band called Holy Holy, with Spiders from Mars drummer Woody Woodmansey and Tony Visconti.

Ian Reddington, another working-class lad, was a former skin-head shod in silver-sprayed Doc Martens, wearing a black Crombie overcoat. He landed the role of the Herald in *Marat/Sade* with no previous acting experience, went on to train at RADA and the RSC and was watched by millions on *Coronation Street* and *East Enders*.

Martyn Ware and Phil Oakey, two of the founders of The Human League (Martyn later went on to form Heaven 17) were boyfriends of two of my best friends at school. I was in love with a drummer for most of this period. Trust me when I say never take any career advice from me. I told him I didn't think The Human League would ever really make it.

Meatwhistle taught me about creating my own life; about the power of agency. We were all in a way joy seekers, working out how to be happy, practising for life. It, and Sheffield, probably saved me, though at the time I didn't realise it.

While all of this was going on, my brother would be watching the stars at night, taking motorbikes apart and putting them back together in the old barn at Slade Hooton Hall, driving his beloved angry-noise motocross bikes, and trying to avoid my father. He had lots of friends in Sheffield too, but he seemed to prefer to stay at home more. David as a teenager was already sinking amidst the downs and occasional highs of our family, but because I was running away most of the time, I didn't notice.

●

This evening, my mother cooks sausages under the eye-level gas grill, chips in the deep fat fryer, and there'll be ice cream for dessert. I have bad acne throughout my teens. She calls us down to eat, shouting at the bottom of the stairs, 'Helen, David, dinner!' We take our time to come down, reluctance weighting down our steps.

I shall judge how much my father has had to drink before deciding whether or not to give him my still-sealed school report. Two of his gin and tonics equal at least four ordinary doubles and might have been enough to take the edge off.

We sit down at the table, chairs scraping on the cold tiled floor, and have a slice of bread and butter. My father pours himself a glass of wine and then one for my mother. We are nearly through with the sausages, heated-up frozen peas and frozen chips, with brown Daddies sauce or tomato ketchup, when I say quietly, 'My school report came today.'

'Well bring it over, I may as well see it,' my father says. 'Let's hope it's a good one.'

'Me too,' I say. Best be positive. He tears open the envelope and reads, in silence.

'Not an inspiring set of results, Helen. And what's this? "Helen is too independently minded. She must learn to conform more", is what Miss Lutz says.'

Our headmistress, Miss Lutz, is inevitably called Miss Lust at school, but trying a joke here would be terrible timing.

'I'm spending all that money on your school fees and you come back with a report like this. You could do better, Helen. It won't do.'

'But what she's really complaining about is the fact that Nicola Bower and me want to set up an upper third drama group. It's crazy. It would be such a great thing for them but all Miss Lutz can see is problems. She hates us trying anything new! And we only want to put on *The Importance of Being Earnest*. Not exactly revolutionary, is it? But she says there'd be a problem about the toilets, that we can't have the fathers going to our toilets, as it's a girls' school.'

At this my mother stands up and looks at my father. She raises her voice and says, 'No, you can't say that.' We all three look at her. She never confronts my father.

'You're wrong. Helen needs independence, her independence of spirit. It's what will get her through her life. It's what counts,' my mum blurts out. I feel a little internal surge in my heart. Thank you, Mum.

'Well,' my father says, clearing his throat. 'Your mother has had her say. But I don't want to have to look at any more reports like this.'

'Please may I get down from the table?'

'May I too?' asks David.

'Yes,' says my father, still looking stunned. 'Once you've cleared away your plates and put them in the dishwasher.' We do so as quickly as possible and skedaddle out of the kitchen to safer zones.

'What about your report?' I ask David.

'He didn't ask, so I won't say anything. No point.'

I walk the dog again and my brother goes back to fiddle with his motorbikes. Mum later takes to her bed with a migraine. This will probably take at least a couple of days to go away and, in the meantime, we'll need to keep quiet.

When my father is back conducting and drinking in the drawing room, whisky now, I sneak a look at my school report, left out on the table. There are six A minuses in there, for English Literature, History, French, Maths, Geography and Greek, my favourite subjects. Sheffield High School for Girls, set up about a hundred years ago, (motto: 'Knowledge is now no more a fountain sealed') doesn't believe in awarding As because 'nothing is ever perfect'. Even Agnes Simms, who does everything easily and perfectly and completes her homework on the bus home, only gets straight A minuses.

●

David was an explorer, an experimenter, a dreamer, an inventor. He could crumple under my father's iron gaze, but still carried on doing what he liked doing. As a teenager he attended King Edwards, the boys' grammar school opposite mine, where my father had been head boy and won a classics scholarship to Cambridge before him. This fact did David no favours. He was often compared to his father and fell short:

'You're no chip off the old block!' He slipped from As to Bs and lower as he progressed up the school, refusing to do anything different like work harder. He failed his exams at his polytechnic later on – maybe he thought that he would show Dad he was different. Either that or he reckoned he would maybe get away with not working one way or another.

He learned to stonewall inside the house while outside everything throbbed, growled and roared. He learned more about motocross bikes than almost anyone, except his friends the two Robs and Christopher, racing them and recording best times industriously. I just kept wondering why it was that everything about boys had to be a competition.

One of the Robs later opened a successful motorbike shop locally. No one in our family would ever

David, aged 17,
Slade Hooton Hall

have thought that could be an option for my brother: the focus was always on what David was failing to do rather than what he loved. I still feel guilty for not protecting him from my father as much as I should, although these days I know that was not my job.

I wish I could remember more happy times. There must have been good times and laughter, not just when other people were around, watching, when my parents behaved better. I would love to be able to say, like other people do, 'I had a happy childhood'. But maybe if we'd been happy in Slade Hooton it would have been worse when the really bad thing happened. Maybe I wouldn't have survived unless I'd been out on the windy ridge in the Spartan cold. But then again, if we hadn't been out on the windy ridge and we had been happy, the really bad thing would never have happened.

Chapter 9

Early March 1981, 13 Albion Place, Doncaster

I lie awake until the sun tries to break through clouded skies at about 6.30 a.m., when sleep finally drags me down. I start up at 8 a.m., the bell on my old red Mickey Mouse alarm clock ringing. I bang the button on the top to make it stop as I've done thousands of times before. Nowadays when I surface I'm still in the crater: no blissful second of not knowing what's different.

My mother must be downstairs in the kitchen; her slippers shuffle on the floor below. I hope she has a dressing gown on. My mother can walk around our house, even the garden, semi-naked. I'm still not used to it. My friends marvel at how liberal my parents are.

I pull the bedclothes over my head and turn over, feeling a yearning tug inside. I need Cleo, need to bury my head into her fur and stroke her silky tan ears. If a dog's natural default mode is happiness, Cleo's is joy. She won't mind if I cry. I'll collect her today.

Cleo, the gordon setter

The thought lifts me just enough that I can get out of bed, pull on yesterday's clothes, go to the loo and splash water on my face without looking in the mirror. The telephone rings again, jarringly. My parents moved into this house a couple of years ago and there is still only one telephone, in the kitchen.

As I head downstairs I see a large, male shape outside the glazed front door ahead and for a moment, my heart leaps. 'David!'

My father opens the door and steps inside with today's *Daily Telegraph* under his arm. He nods towards me, closes the door, and we move together towards the kitchen to reach the phone before my mother.

Mum has her dressing gown on. She sits on a stool, her back to the kitchen table, looking out of the window.

'Hello. Geoffrey Garlick speaking.' He usually picks up like this, though sometimes, it is just 'Garlick speaking'. We have all forgotten this was ever funny.

'Yes, yes. My daughter and I were planning to come over later on. She just flew back from St Louis. From America,' he clarifies.

I walk over to be in front of him and mouth, 'I want to get Cleo.'

He shakes his head in irritation; turns away. He listens, unusually, for a long while, nodding his head firmly in short bursts from time to time, pressing his lips together, his breaths coming quicker until he finally erupts.

'Look, now, listen to me, never mind *resources*. This is top priority. We, the family, need to get the bottom of who's done this. Frankly, that's your job. What about that cotton bobbin key fob? I'd never seen it before. Have you tested it for fingerprints? What exactly have you tested?' A pause, while he listens.

'Yes, yes I can get there. Half an hour or so should do it. It's been nearly a week. The evidence is getting cold, there have been so many people in the Hall already, tramping up and down, we're losing time.' He presses on. 'This is my son we're talking about. I must get to the bottom of who killed him, I won't forgive myself if I don't. Never mind anyone else.' He lashes down the receiver.

'Was that the police?' I ask, pointlessly.

'Bloody idiots. Christ. They don't know what they're doing. Absolutely useless.' He walks over to the kettle and slams it on the stove, spilling water.

My mother gets up from the stool and silently takes the kettle from him, checks it, fills it up more and places it back on the stove. 'Tea or coffee?' she asks, looking down. 'I'm going to the market in a bit to get us some food for tonight.' She reaches up for the mugs.

The phone rings again; my father answers.

'Hello, Garlick speaking. Ah. It's good of you to call, Jeremy.' Jeremy – or Jem – Parsons is the vicar for St Marwenne's in Marhamchurch; my brother will be buried in the churchyard there. You'd never pick Jem out as a vicar if it weren't for the dog collar. His hair, slightly lank, grows below the dog collar and falls over his sideburns. He has a rather pointed nose and full cheeks set in a long face, and wears spectacles with thick black frames. My parents have often told me it would be a good idea for me to marry Jem, though neither Jem nor I have shown any inclination.

My father puts his hand over the receiver.

'Do you mind if I take this call? It might take me a while. Helen, you come over here with me, there are things we'll need to discuss,' my father says. I sit next to him on a kitchen stool to listen in to the call. Mum heads back to the sitting room to have her coffee. I nod to my father to show I'm ready. He takes his hand away from the receiver and continues.

'Thank you for calling me back, especially so early in the morning. I thought it would be good to get a few matters settled, Jem, ahead of our coming down to Marhamchurch and there were a couple of things I need to run past you. First, I thought it would be fitting for David's friends to carry the coffin. One of them has volunteered already. I personally would rather it was they who were carrying their friend rather than any anonymous pallbearers.'

'You'll need six, really.' Jem speaks firmly, I can hear him.

'I'm not sure who it would be at this stage. Would four suffice, do you think?'

He looks over at me. I shrug, not sure what to say.

He continues, 'I believe four of the lads are willing. They're strong. You'll know them I think from the cricket team, Jem. I imagine that it's something they'd want to do for David: a fitting tribute.'

Jem seems now to say something noncommittal at the other end of the line. I lean in a bit more to hear him.

'So we'll proceed with four?' My father doesn't wait for an answer. 'I also wanted to mention that we don't yet have a date for the inquest. I'm sure it will be just a formality, to confirm it was an accident. We're burying David, of course, so once the coroner releases his body, that wouldn't need to hold up the funeral?'

'That's not a problem, Geoffrey. Would you like to come over to the rectory when you're down at the Salt Box?' Jem responds. 'We can discuss the funeral arrangements in the round. Best to get these things sorted out, then that will be off your mind.'

'That's kind, father,' says my father, slipping into calling Jem 'father', which he does sometimes, to mark his status as an Anglican priest. Dad is genuinely grateful.

People have already started lining up into two camps. One supports his version of the accident and the other talks of the terrible thing of his son killing himself. Only those who tell my father how sorry they are about the accident remain in the inner circle. I have to keep my counsel more. I'm constantly editing myself in case something slips out that he doesn't want to hear. You wouldn't want to cross my father.

'Another thing, about the undertakers. I want it dug deep, enough not only for David but also Monica and myself, and Helen. Can you organise that, or would you like me to contact them?'

'Of course.' Jem's tone is reassuring. 'Geoffrey, I also wanted to let you know something, which might help. I recalled that I last saw David and his friend Nick Cain in the Bullers Arms one night not long ago. I believe it was a jazz evening, sometime last month. It was windy, I remember that. Nick might have been kind enough to buy me a drink, after I'd offered to buy a round for them. David said he was a bit skint: that old story. He was his usual self. They were both laughing, quite chatty. It was light hearted, you know, sport, matters of local interest, nothing weighty. David seemed perfectly fit and contented: as relaxed as ever.'

My father's brow furrows and I see tears in his green eyes.

'You might have been one of the last people to see David alive, Jem.' Dad pauses. 'I don't mind telling you, how difficult it might be showing that David was without a care. It is hard proving a no, don't you find?'

'I don't really get involved in that kind of thing but if it would ever help at all, of course I'd be willing to write a letter confirming my meeting with David and his state of mind at that time,' the vicar ventured.

'Well, thank you, father. You appreciate that this may have to be put to a coroner. There is a chance you would be asked to come in person to give evidence at any inquest, although I doubt it. Any letter wouldn't need to be long, just the main facts.'

'It's just that I'm not sure of the date.'

'Let me look at the diary. Helen, pass it to me would you? Now, Jem, you mentioned that jazz was on at the Bullers – isn't that on Wednesdays? I think it must have been February the eighteenth, a

Wednesday. It can't have been the week before because we were having dinner with David then, and the week after he was back in Bothamsall.'

'That was most likely the day. You let me know if you need me to write a letter and I'll get it off to you in early course. I'll write it on my St Marwenne's headed notepaper.'

'That's very kind of you.'

'And I'll see you both, and Helen, when you next come down. Is that all for now, Geoffrey?'

'Yes, thank you. I'll need to talk to you about the gravestone but I want to talk that through with the family first. Goodbye then, Jem.'

'Bye, Geoffrey. All the very best to you and Monica, and Helen of course.'

I am left pondering whether Jem, a bachelor without children, a shy man despite being often found in the pub, would have been able to identify what my brother's underlying state of mind was. Were any of us? Were we all in a way just pretending, hoping that things were better or would at least get better because that let us off the hook? My father and Jem, with their common interests in cricket and literature and shared love of music, albeit different forms, enjoyed each other's company and had spent much time together setting up a new cricket ground and team for the village, a project inspired by Jem's discovery of an old cricket pitch in the field by the rectory. Jem would want to help, in whatever way he could, and not just spiritually. But I am in survival mode, in a haze of pain. I have barely enough energy to get through a day never mind figure out what's really going on.

Minutes later, my father and I are in the car and on the road to Bothamsall Hall. Focus on Cleo, I keep thinking. When my mind strays to anything else, my heartbeat pounds so much it hurts to breathe and I think it would be almost easier not to. I won't go inside if he asks me to, I can't, I promise myself.

My father turns on the car radio. It's Radio 4, the *Today* programme, John Timpson and Brian Redhead, a scrap of comfortable familiarity. There is an item about Diana Spencer, who stepped out in a black lace décolletage dress on the arm of Prince Charles the day my brother died. Media attention is growing.

·

Monica hears the front door click shut behind her husband and her surviving child. She waits, in case Geoffrey has forgotten anything, then hears the Daimler drive away, its low purr louder than usual. She exhales, thinking, Geoffrey's driving too fast. Please don't let them have an accident.

Alone, she lets herself break down. Punching a tapestry cushion she embroidered years ago, she pulls it into her face to scream, 'Why?' without the neighbours hearing her. She feels scrutinised by them, everyone, her mother, her sister, even Geoffrey and her daughter. Judgement weighs in their eyes. It is her fault, the ballast is in that. But the truth is different. It was her husband who never really understood his son.

She cries so much that she ends up vomiting, and has to rush into the bathroom to try and spew out the misery. Being sick will make you feel better, that's what she said to her children in the past, although she wasn't sure if she believed it, and she hated sick. It doesn't help her today.

She feels trapped in the life she had to choose all those years ago, because her mother gave her an ultimatum: 'Get married, or get out.' Her punishment now is worse than anyone should ever have to bear.

Monica is not used to making a lot of noise, even stifled like this. She deliberately slows her breathing to stop herself from her crying. It hasn't helped. I won't do that again, she resolves. She has history in making up her mind about something.

She goes upstairs, forcing herself to have a shower and get dressed. She wears baggy trousers, big pants, a saggy tee shirt, no bra, flat shoes. She drinks half a glass of water, wishing it was whisky. She takes two Valium.

Monica decides to call her best friend Gwen, a matron at the Doncaster Royal Infirmary. She has a feeling it might be Gwen's day off. She doesn't let herself call Gwen often, but she must today.

Gwen picks up on the second ring. 'Hello. Gwen Dowson speaking.'

Monica can't bring herself to say anything. That familiar voice, known for over thirty years, its sternness masking humour just beneath the surface.

'Pip, is that you?' Gwen asks.

'Of course it's me.'

'How are you, my love?' Gwen asks.

'I don't know how I can get through even the next hour, Gwen. I'm in hell, like my mother cursed me. You remember?'

'Yes I do. Clear as day. Poor Pip. I can't imagine what you're going through.'

'No. I don't expect you can.'

'How is Geoffrey, and Helen?'

'I can't stand it. He weeps and wails. He keeps going on about it being an accident. I can hardly look at him.'

'Poor Geoffrey.'

'Shut up. Helen's here now, back from the States. She's gone off with him this morning, back to that place. And Geoffrey says he doesn't "do" divorce.'

'Has it got that bad? Have you said that's what you want to do?'

Pip is silent.

'How can I help? What do you want me to do?' Gwen asks, gently.

'Nothing. Nothing helps. Anyway, I can't ever leave him now.'

'I can see that. But you'll have each other for comfort. And Helen.'

'Will you be there? At the funeral?' Pip pleads.

'I'll come to the Laughton one, if it's what you both want, and I'm well enough. I don't want to make anything worse for you. It's a memorial service, isn't it?'

'That's the idea, but we haven't planned it all yet. We've still got to wait for the coroner to release his body. And I'm so tired. Oh God. I'm exhausted.'

'I'm so sorry, Pip.'

'Yes, that's what people say if they say anything. A lot of people avoid me. It's as if it's catching.'

'Pip, I must tell you something else, give you some notice. I don't know if there's a right time to say it, but I can't get down to Cornwall for the proper funeral. I've had too many days off at work. Maud also thinks it would not be a good idea for me to come. And I can't get compassionate leave, you're not family. I'm sorry I can't be there for you. I will be there for the Laughton memorial service.'

Monica puts the phone down without saying goodbye. Everyone lets her down. And that bloody Maud, Gwen doesn't seem to be able to make her own decisions any more since that skinny little woman started living with her.

She pulls down her coat from the rack, pushes her left hand through one sleeve and then twists round to find the second arm: the movement hurts. She then puts the strap of her navy blue handbag over her usual shoulder, the right, then reconsiders and puts it over her head. It sits like a satchel on her body, the strap tightening crossways over her camel coat. It holds her together more. She pulls a knitted grey hat over her head, covering every strand of blond. Before she goes out, she takes her lipstick from her bag and puts on Sunkiss, the first time since Geoffrey found David, but her daughter is back now.

She rolls her shopping trolley from the cupboard under the stairs, out of the front door, giving herself an almost imperceptible shake. She could go the longer way around to the fish market, up South Parade, turning right by the Gaumont, then third right off Thorne Road to stop off at her mother's house in Lawn Road, but she won't. Since her father died just over four years ago, it is even more of an ordeal to visit her mother.

Monica checks her watch. It's nearing 10 a.m. Once her mother's had her Horlicks and an orange, halved and slurped for breakfast, she'll be popping the cork of today's bottle of Anjou rosé. No point trying to talk to Madge between 10.30 a.m. and 3.30 p.m. Her record will soon be playing once again, 'My mother was an angel sent from heaven, my father was the devil incarnate'.

Her eyes glance again at the little gold-plated watch. Its expandable metal strap catches at the hairs on her wrist. It was Geoffrey's birthday present for her last November. 'Next year, when you're fifty, we'll get you something special,' he'd promised.

She hasn't much liked wearing it before. Now she puts it on every day. The pain from the delicate wrist hairs it pinches out feels like something real. She thinks that she won't wear any other jewellery in future, apart from her wedding ring. It would cause too much consternation if she took that off. She hears the telephone starting up again as she's closing the door, and she pulls it firmly shut behind her.

Monica now recalls, from deep within the cave where she now lives, that cordon bleu course she did years back; it was a better time.

If she can get a meal on the table, it will be an achievement. That becomes her plan. Maybe piquant prawns.

She puts one foot in front of the other, counting out her paces, making slow progress down the pathway, with almost a glimmer of a purpose, into the grey day.

Chapter 10

My father is driving too fast as we head out of Doncaster. Neither he nor I have a seat belt on. My parents say it's more dangerous to try and get out of a car after an accident if you've been strapped in. 'It's not worth the risk,' they say.

'Dad, careful.' I motion towards the speedometer.

He is about to snap back but holds himself in check. 'How did you sleep? We've been thinking about you so much while you were away. You will tell us about your time in America.'

'I will, but let's do whatever we've got to do first. What's happening?'

'I can't believe it. The police hadn't checked fully for fingerprints, apparently the DCI had previously said they didn't need to. I've had a word with them. They said that they are taking witness statements, they're going to see Bill, Cleo is staying with him at the moment, did I tell you that? And they've interviewed the chap next door, a teacher I think he is, he might know something or might have heard something. I mean, surely he would have heard the gun go off, you'd think, wouldn't you?'

'But where did the gun come from? It can't have been just lying around?' I ask. There are several seconds of silence. My father is looking at the road ahead, then his eyes move to the rear-view mirror.

He says, almost to himself, 'That bloody cabinet, if he hadn't left that open.' My father now looks out of his side window and the car starts drifting to the right.

'Dad!' I call out. A red lorry is fast approaching in the opposite lane. He yanks his head to look in front and swerves his car back to the left, just in time. The lorry driver silently shouts at my father behind his window, jamming his hand on his horn. The horn screams loud then lessens as we move nearer to where my brother died.

'Why do you think he did it?' I can't stop myself. 'Daddy, I worry it's because I went to the States and David was too lonely. It was my fault for going away.'

My father shoots me a brief look, before facing forward to where he's heading.

'Helen you mustn't think that. It's not possible. When your mother and I last saw him, he was much more like himself,' my father says, in his echo chamber. 'It must have been an intruder. I'd never seen that key with the cotton bobbin on it, for example.'

'Christmas wasn't exactly …' I trail off, remembering unspoken warfare, slammed doors, harsh looks, drinking starting at 11a.m., loud clashing plates, a slurred toast, lunch served up just after the Queen's speech, pretend jollity over cracker jokes, my brother barely being able to stand being in a room with any other members of the family and going to his bedroom whenever he decently could. We were physically together, but mentally running off in different directions.

'Your mother and I thought it would do your brother good to go down to Cornwall, be with his friends, after he'd left Bothamsall. You knew he was due to leave on the tenth of March? We encouraged him: he'd got it mapped out. The cricket season's not far off, he might have got a job for the summer. And there's that friend of his, Nick. The vicar called and said he'd seen David and Nick together a few days before and David was his usual sunny self. He'll write me a letter, Jem will – oh, but you know that, of course. David was always happier down at the Salt Box.'

'That's true. Tell me more about what happened when you and Mum last saw him?'

'Nothing that much to report. We went over to Bothamsall, your mother had cooked shepherd's pie and she took out her apple pie from the freezer, with ice cream, I know it's winter but David likes ice cream.' He goes quiet. 'Liked.' He pauses.

'There was no indication Helen, nothing. Smiles, chatting about the footie, how Wednesday were doing in the league, motorbikes, his friends from Sheffield now at university. Where you were. You hadn't sent a postcard for ages. I didn't know what was going on with you, although I thought you'd be all right. But we didn't really talk about you.'

He pauses. 'It was just a night having dinner, an ordinary night. He was in good form. I said see you soon, after we're back on the 27th. "All right, Dad," he said. We hugged each other when I left.'

'I bet that hadn't happened for a while.' I can't stop myself, and I don't even believe it anyway.

My father starts to break down. He cries in staccato sobs, ripping out of him, with a 'hhhuuur' sound at the end. I freeze and can't find anything to say. I wonder if I'll need to take over driving. Then he pulls himself together, his breathing becomes more regular, and we continue on the road towards Bothamsall Hall.

'Oh, and I mentioned about the gravestone. Your mother and I thought it would be best if we had it made from York stone. More appropriate for David. He was from Yorkshire, after all. He could have even played for the Yorkshire cricket team, you know, being born in the county.'

'OK.'

'And I just wanted to put on it his full name, date of birth and …' he pauses. 'When he died. And then 'Sometime of Slade Hooton

Hall', do you have any objection? There will be plenty of space on the gravestone for all of our names, later on.'

He carries on talking about the arrangements and I try to tune out. I think it's mad to put 'Sometime of Slade Hooton Hall', but I can't face the thought of another battle and maybe this will give him some comfort.

It's an unfamiliar journey and I look out of the window.

When we head into Bothamsall Hall, I think back to when my parents must have swung through these gates on 1st March. I feel a twinge of resentment towards my brother, though no way would I admit it. If he hadn't done this, we wouldn't all be falling apart. I wouldn't have sole responsibility for my parents; everything would be better.

My dad parks his car and looks at me. 'Will you come in?'

I'm often squeamish, fainting if I have to have an injection or even visit someone in hospital: the blood rushes out of my head and I wake up on the floor. What I thought I would say is, 'Dad, I can't go inside.'

Bothamsall Hall

I actually say, 'Yes, of course.' Get on with it, I tell myself. Dad opens his car door, closes it behind him and walks towards the back door of the Hall. His shoulders slump down now, his fire extinguished.

I've avoided looking at the Hall so far but my eyes follow his foot-fall. Bothamsall Hall looks washed out: brown, grey and enormous. Dad waits briefly by the door before stepping inside. There are two policemen there and tape to keep people away. Bothamsall village is a small place, I hadn't expected that. But three figures stand by the main gate, looking over. One woman has a scarf tied on her head and an old-fashioned pram with what looks like a toddler sitting up in it, and is with another, older woman – maybe her mother, their stance is similar. Plus a neighbour? As I look towards them, one of the women nudges the other, nodding her head over in our direction. All three of them stare. If I didn't feel nothing inside, I would hate them.

We go in, through the hallway, past a neat pile of things belonging to my brother and into the green room, which looks not just untidy but also unlooked after. Empty bottles of beer and wine are still where my father would have found them, scattered. There is the settee my father described; there is a dried-up brown pool where my brother's head would have been. I want to close my eyes but cannot help seeing streaks like tiny runways on the red lampshade by the sofa. The room is deathly cold and smells of liquorice, old alcohol, tobacco and a sweet, sickly smell – almost like tangerine, but fake, as though from an air freshener. The stench hits me like a sick avalanche and I feel familiar waves of nausea. Where can I sit down? No one has yet cleaned up. My father has told me that will be our job, once the police have gone. I must get my head down before I crash out.

'Just a minute, I'm just going back to the car. I've forgotten something.' The men are all gathered round together and don't seem to notice. I'm not sure they heard me.

I manage to get outside before I faint, and squat down onto the flagged step to put my head between my knees, feeling the stone's cold seep into me. I take deep breaths, before noticing those bloody women again, latter-day French Revolution knitters, staring. As soon as I feel better, I get up and walk into the back garden where no one can watch me. An old wooden seat is at one side of the lawn and I head there.

A robin bobs down to the paving by the seat and looks at me, his head cocked. His breast is startlingly red in the sepia setting. 'I've nothing for you,' I whisper. After a while the robin flies back onto a branch and starts singing. My grannie had told me that a robin's song is a version of, 'Get out, this is my territory and that's my woman', but more beautiful.

I wonder how long I can stretch out being in the garden. But I don't want the ignominy of the police coming out to find me, so after a while I head back into the Hall.

A policeman comes over to say, 'Ah, we thought we might have lost you. You're Geoffrey Garlick's lass?'

'Yes, I am.'

'I'm sorry, love,' he says, almost forgetting himself. 'I've just been speaking with your father. My colleague's doing some testing now.' He motions over to another man, wearing gloves, who looks as if he might be scattering talcum powder over a tabletop. After watching him work, the policeman resumes. 'Would you mind me asking you a few questions to see if you need to make a statement?'

'That's all right. Does my father know?'

'You're over 18? Since 1970 you'll have been considered an adult, Miss Garlick.'

'Yes.'

'Well, there's no problem then. Can I just confirm that at the time of the death of the deceased – sorry, your brother – in Both-amsall, you were abroad?'

'Yes, that's right, I'd been travelling abroad since the sixth of January. I came back as soon as I could,' I said, feeling guilty already.

'Were you in contact with your brother whilst you were away?'

'I'd sent him a postcard or two, but no, I hadn't spoken to him since I left.'

'Is there anything you might know about the circumstances of his death that would help us in our enquiries? Anything he might have said to you?'

'No, n-no,' I stammer. 'I don't think so. I never thought … If I had known this might happen …' I can't stop myself from starting to cry.

I look over to my father. His body language is different, almost supplicating. He's not talking much but nodding mostly, sometimes tangling his fingers around his thinning hair and threading it over his bald patch, his way of comforting himself. He looks back at me and gives me a brief grimace, supposed to reassure me.

'When did you last speak properly with your brother?'

'It would have been just after Christmas. Before I left for America.'

('David, I'm not like Mum and Dad. I want to talk, find out how you are, what's going on?'

'But I don't want to talk to you. I don't want to talk to anyone. You're just like them, anyway. Leave me alone.'

Those may be the last words he spoke to me. He might have added, 'Goodbye,' before he slammed the door shut on me.)

'What did he say?'

'He didn't say much. We were saying goodbye. I can't remember exactly what his last words were, but I imagine he'd have said "goodbye".'

'Do you remember anything about his demeanour then which would have given cause for concern?'

'Not really. No.'

I'm not exactly lying. I'd worried about my brother for years, but in a tucked-into-the-back-of-my-head way. And if I say that I was worried, this would surely lead to more worry for my father, and my mother, who have quite enough problems. Hard as it is to lose a brother, it must be worse for them. He was their child. What could be more devastating?

'Nothing to lead you to believe that he was having unhappy thoughts?'

'I didn't think that, no. He kept himself to himself. He was more into motorbikes and things like that, things I wasn't into. He had lots of friends.'

'How did your brother get on with your father? Your parents?'

'They were away in Cyprus you know, my parents. My dad said he'd seen David just before they left to go on holiday. He said he was happy.'

'Was your brother generally happy, would you say?'

'He was happy when he was younger, always smiling. I think these last few years he hadn't been quite so smiley.' I fall silent, feeling I am somehow betraying my family. 'But there's nothing specific I can tell you.'

The policeman looks at me coolly. 'We're going to take a statement from the man who looks after the dog, as well as anyone else who may have seen the deceased. It is your dog, Cleo, that's her name, isn't it?'

'Yes, she's called Cleo. And she's mine,' I say.

'Your father said that the dog was your brother's,' says the policeman. I shrug.

'I took a statement from the man who lives next door, a school-teacher he is, the day after we were called to the Hall by your father. He hadn't heard anything. If – and it's a big if – anybody else had got into the property, from our enquiries it looks as if that person would have been known to your brother. There was no forced entry. At the moment we're keeping all avenues of enquiry open. And the coroner will be making his decision in due course.'

'OK.'

'By the way, we don't think we need to do more tests on your Renault. You'll be able to pick it up when you want. Maybe today? It's your car?'

I look at him uneasily, not knowing what the right thing is to say.

'I checked the records and saw the car is registered in your name. Your father had told us the car was your brother's.'

'I think my father would have meant that as David was using the car, we all thought it was his for the time being. His car, well he'd had a lot of problems with it. It drank more oil than petrol.'

The policeman snaps his notebook shut.

'Your father's a solicitor of course,' he says. 'It's his duty to tell the truth, though I don't need to tell you that, or him for that matter. We're here to find out what happened.'

I say nothing else. It seems safer.

'Goodbye, then. I'll be in touch if there's anything more we might need from you. This is my number if you want to ring me. If there's anything that comes up, or anything you might have …' he pauses. 'Forgotten.' He hands me a card.

The policeman walks over to his fellow officer, who is with my father, while I stay put. They talk in voices so low that I can't distinguish what they are saying. They look over at me as the officer hands something to my father. My father proffers his hand to shake theirs goodbye. They don't take his hand but instead nod and move back, deeper into the room.

My father comes towards me. I am worried about whether he'll be angry with me. Maybe I should have said that I was planning to transfer the name in the log-book to David?

'They've confirmed they don't need to take a formal statement from you, Helen. You can't add anything. If I was you, I'd get off now, take the car and go and collect Cleo. Here are the car keys,' he says, handing them to me.

'What about Mum? She can't stand Cleo.'

'She'll be all right. It would do you good to have Cleo. Give you something else to think about. I've spoken to the police. They said they have taken some fingerprints at least. They don't think there's been a break-in, though how can anyone be sure of that unless they were there?' He pauses.

'Helen, I think your mother and I are going to go down to the Salt Box as soon as we can, so long as the police don't need me anymore. There are arrangements to be made. As soon as they release the body, I want us to give David a decent funeral. He'll be buried in the churchyard where he can look out towards the sea.' He can't stop himself from crying again.

'Bye, Dad. Drive carefully.'

The *tricoteuses* are still there, and the toddler is wailing. One of the women shouts at the toddler. 'Shuddup. Put that dummy in yer mouth.' Cold comfort.

Apart from them, I am alone as I head over to my little yellow car, not driven by me since January. I walk round the car twice, pretending to check it. The last person to drive it would have been my brother. I tell myself that the policemen will have opened up the car and dusted it for evidence, checked the dashboard, looked through the things that David's hand would previously have touched, so the thread is broken anyway.

I so want him here with me. I want to ask him what on earth he's been doing and see him shrug and his smile like the sun coming out from behind a cloud. It's unending, this hunger for all the things that we had and would have had together. I remember us racing out, with our painted surfboards, mine orange, David's blue, into the sea's edge in Widemouth Bay and screaming with joy and shock as the waves hit us, my mum not far behind us, with her own dark-varnished board. Imagine him smiling at me as I walk down some aisle; holding my future child; helping me with our parents as they age. He might not have been easy as a teenager but surely we would have got back to the way it once was when we were close, wouldn't we? If he had lived?

I get into the car, pull the door shut, sit down, check that the gearstick underneath the steering wheel is in neutral, and put the key in the ignition. Then pause. I breathe out, feeling safer alone. I shall drive over to collect the only living being I trust for comfort. All the humans seem somehow at fault. David's death has shone a searchlight on to our family, on everyone. We are all asking 'What if' questions.

Before I turn the key I catch the smell of my brother, unmistakeable. An earthy mix of maleness: sweat, motorbike oil, beer, mud, fishing, Lynx, fresh air. My brother smelled like nobody else. My little brother, whom I'd grown up with and had baths with and fed when he was little and who had an imaginary friend called Sowundee and who used to hug me under the bedclothes, hiding from the ghosts. I am a little afraid, but can't help smiling. It's my brother after all. I feel a cool brush of air on my face.

I put the car into reverse, while saying hello. It feels rude not to acknowledge him. I drive back to Slade Hooton to collect my canine comfort blanket from Bill.

Bill tells me the police have been round and they have said they want to interview him and his next-door neighbour's sons. While he talks, I treasure Cleo's black and tan head resting on my lap, stroke her silky ears and look into her dark brown eyes, her gaze fixed on my face. She soothes me. My breathing steadies a little, even as Bill tells me that when David dropped Cleo off in the village, he didn't stop.

Chapter 11

WILLIAM [████████] SWORN SAITH :-

I live at [████████████] Slade Hooton Laughton Near Sheffield. I am a retired Colliery Official.

I have lived at my present address for eight years and during this time I got to know a Mr and Mrs Garlick who until 18 months ago lived at Slade Hooton Hall.

On many occasions I would keep Mr Garlick's dog for him when he went away. The dog is a black and tan Gordon setter.

Mr Garlick had a son, David Garlick, and I understand that in October 1980 David went to look after a Hall near Retford. David took with him the Gordon setter which is called 'Cleo'.

In February this year I received a letter from Mrs Garlick, David's mother. She informed me that David would have to leave the Hall he was looking after because its owner would be returning from abroad on March 10th 1981 and therefore David would be bringing Cleo for me to look after if possible. I wrote back to Mrs Garlick and informed her that I was prepared to take Cleo back.

Around midday on Saturday 21st February 1981, I was working at The Cottage Slade Hooton where I do some gardening. A boy who lives near us, Dale [████████] who is only 8 or 9 years old, came to see me at The Cottage. Dale [████████] told me that Cleo was back. I thought he was pulling my leg but then I saw the dog playing in the garden of The Cottage. I thought it was very odd that

David Garlick had not even bothered to find me in the village and had apparently just left the dog in the village.

I always found David Garlick to be a likeable person. He was always polite, and I got on with him very well. I think he worried a little about losing his hair but I don't know much about that.

I really was surprised that he didn't bother to find me before leaving Cleo in the village.

Over the past four years I have looked after Cleo quite a lot and so I'm sure Dale [████████] would know the dog quite well. One other thing that was odd about David Garlick's behaviour was that on every occasion he has brought me Cleo before he has always left me a load of dog food and if I've not been in, he's left things in my garage.

I am certain of the date being 21st February 1981 as I have checked my diary and found an entry I made on that date stating simply, 'Cleo returned.'

Statement of	Craig [████████]
Age	10 years
Occupation	Schoolboy
Address	[████████]

Dated the 29th day of March 1981

states I am a schoolboy attending Laughton Council school and I reside at the above address with my parents, two brothers and my grandfather.

I can't remember exactly which Saturday it was but I think it's about four weeks ago.

It was sometime in the morning towards dinnertime.

I walked out of our home with my younger brother Dale, 7 years.

We walked onto the road and I saw a yellow Renault 5 car being driven by a man with gingerish hair. The car was coming from the direction of the Abbey and there was a black and brown dog in the back seat of the car.

Dale left me and went off to see a friend and I went into the house next door to see my friend.

My friend wasn't in so I came out of the house straight away.

I looked down the road and saw my brother Dale.

Dale had a black and brown dog following him and I could see a yellow Renault 5 car being driven away towards Maltby.

I recognised the dog that was following Dale as Cleo a dog that is owned by Mr Garlick's daughter.

Mr and Mrs Garlick used to live in Slade Hooton Hall near my home and I used to see Cleo quite a lot and anyway my uncle Bill who lives next door but one used to look after Cleo quite a lot whilst Mr and Mrs Garlick were away.

Mr Garlick's daughter had a yellow Renault 5 car when she lived in Slade Hooton Hall that's why I could recognise the make of the yellow car I saw that day.

That's all I saw that day because after that I went into our house.

29th March 1981

3.07 pm.

[████████] Slade Hooton

Record of conversation between Dale [█████], 7 years, born

[███████████], and DC Ashworth in the presence of Mr [██████]
(father) & DCI Hodgson

DC Ashworth	'Dale, can you remember a man in a yellow car dropping a dog off near your home one day?'
Dale	'Yes, I was going to see my friend, Charles.'
DC Ashworth	'Did the man in the yellow car stop and speak to you?'
Dale	'No, he just stopped the car and opened a door and Cleo jumped out.'
DC Ashworth	'Who is Cleo?'
Dale	'He's a dog that my Uncle Bill looks after for Mr Garlick.'
DC Ashworth	'So what did you do?'
Dale	'Well my Uncle Bill was gardening for Charles's mummy so when I saw Uncle Bill, I told him Cleo was back.'
DC Ashworth	'Did you see Uncle Bill straight away after Cleo had been left in the village?'
Dale	'Oh yes.'
DC Ashworth	'So you know Cleo very well do you?'
Dale	'Yes, we've often fed her for Uncle Bill and she's been to our house a lot.'
DC Ashworth	'Thank you Dale, that's helped me a lot.'

3.16 p.m.	Conversation ended

Chapter 12

My parents and I, and David too, had driven down to Marhamchurch from Yorkshire dozens of times. We headed there most holidays, on the old Fosse way. The car smelled of the boiled eggs, apples, orange squash and fish paste sandwiches already packed. If it was Easter we might get a hot cross bun.

My father would almost always drive the longest but my mother would take over for an hour or so to give Dad a rest. My mother was the better driver, in fact, and drove more smoothly than my father who would rev the accelerator so often we ended up lurching rather than driving. He'd also sometimes miss the turns. We would play I spy and who could spot the sea first – if you won you got a silver sixpence – and we'd have to shut up in the meantime, too. Being quiet was always important. I used to love looking for the ponies on Dartmoor when we drove over the hills. On the way my parents would always stop for lunch at the same pub in Devon and go and get us pasties and half a pint of cider to share while they ate inside. One thing had changed. The M5 motorway's completion in 1977 heralded an end to driving through Lichfield: a big relief. When I drive down to Cornwall it now takes much less than the eight to ten hours it used to. My parents have driven down a day or two before.

A granite house with a Cornish slate roof, the Salt Box was named by the owner, two before my parents, reputedly a sailor. A classic salt-box shape – three windows at the top, two windows below and the door, painted light blue, bang in the middle – it was rendered and painted white on three sides, to protect against the sea-borne wind and rain. A box hedge on stage left was my job to keep trimmed. I liked the task as I got to know people who would stop and chat as they headed to the village shop further along the road.

The Salt Box was once a cobbler's and before that a sweet-shop: customers would enter at the back gate to walk through to the shop. A lowish white-painted wall kept the customers away from the garden and its apple trees. Rusting metal shoe lasts were dug up in the garden. The scullery attached to the kitchen had thick horizontal slabs of slate built into the walls to cool down the boiled sweets and fudge which the shop owner made. She was rumoured to have a temper. One day she fell on the stove where she made her sweets and stuck there with a boiling toffee mix and sizzled to death. That was the story anyway.

Wooden stairs to the first floor led straight up from the front door – or, of course straight down, if you were upstairs already. Many people fell down those stairs, whether through alcohol or a sneaky shove from the sweet-maker's ghost.

My father would tap an old brass barometer next to the front door with his middle fingernail when he went in or out of the door, looking for signs of the weather being set fair. 'Look, it's on the way up,' he would say, 'again.' The annual rainfall in nearby Bude is nowadays 932 mm; the national English average is 885 mm. It would not have been much different then, though his prediction could still have been true. When my parents were at the Salt Box the weather was, more often than not, good: 'You've brought the sun with you,' people in the village told them.

By the end of the seventies, we had locally acquired semi-emmet status. Emmet in Cornish means ant, and describes the swarms of tourists on these bleak beautiful shores in summer. To be considered semi-emmet was an honour.

Most Christmases David and I were ill. We would spend Christmas in bed in the yellow-painted twin-bedded room we shared, which overlooked St Marwenne's church and the sea in the distance, and thus faced into the wind. It was one of the damper rooms of the house. We had measles, mumps, flu, chicken pox, German measles. It was safer up there than downstairs: storms simmered when my parents were together. In summer my father would alternate between spending two weeks in the office and two weeks at the Salt Box. The two weeks he was not there were more peaceful. We read books at the table. David read Marvel comics (his favourite was the Incredible Hulk), or books on whatever interest he currently had: trout fishing, collecting birds' eggs, telescopes, motocross. My mother and I each read several books a week. She, and sometimes David, planted peas, radishes, lettuce and beans in the vegetable garden behind the house and I clipped the box hedge by the front door. David would sometimes get up early and go fishing for river trout, bring them back, gut them and grill them deliciously with butter for breakfast. Life seemed easier without my father.

When David was a bit older, he moved into the smaller bedroom which overlooked the road to Bude. He had to spend a lot of time there one Easter, after he'd broken his leg on the first day of the school ski-ing holiday. The house stood proud at the top of Pinch Hill, the steep road up from Bude, along a road which led from the church to its left down to the village shop and the pub, the Bullers Arms, to its right. According to feng shui principles, that meant the house was unlucky as it would have bad chi from the cars heading straight towards it. It was a loved house, in a much loved village, but I would never describe it as lucky.

Chapter 13

April 1981, Marhamchurch

Trees don't often grow tall in North Cornwall, preferring the sanctuary of valleys where the wind terrorises them less. Their cousins on exposed hillsides, bent back, with their lichened branches like hair streaming out behind, rarely aspire to the heavens.

Today, the trees in the graveyard of St Marwenne's, on the ridge where the horse chestnut grows, under which my brother will soon be buried, are being wind-battered. There will be another funeral, what my parents call a memorial service, in Laughton-en-le-Morthern church later on. More people will come to the memorial service as it's nearer for them, so there are fewer mourners in Cornwall, where David is going to be buried.

The rooks in the trees are being lashed around, cawing and fighting not to be tossed in the wind. Pewtery rolls of rain clouds press down to narrow the gateway between earth and … well … let's just call it the next stage. Umbrellas turn out to be useless: those brought by mourners are whipped inside out.

Driving rain spears into my face, but I don't mind. I have always loved the wind and storms; they remind me of freedom. Blow winds, and bloody well crack your cheeks. Make me feel so damn cold that I am forced to think about something other than the void; the crater inside. Each step takes me to a place where I can no longer pretend that he is not dead.

I see my parents bowed with grief, pulled towards the earth. My mother's beautiful lips, now pinched, try to smile, though the attempt never gets to her eyes. She has a set script if she says anything at all. 'Thank you for coming.'

I recall the echoes of her cries through her bedroom wall last night. Mum, as if withered to only half the mum she was, is continuing to take Valium. If it works a bit in the light, in the night it loses its grip.

My father cries more, though his crying barely escapes him. He keeps swallowing and gulping back his tears. He watches my mother, usually with sideways glances, as if his life depends on her. I find it hard to feel much sympathy for him, and my anger at how he treated my brother since he was a teenager simmers. Most of the time, though, I blame myself for David's death: by not being there, it was my fault. Were I still in the same country, maybe he would have opened up to me about the dark place he must have been heading into.

We survivors are not in this together. We are wide apart, not close. Not comforted or comforting, just enduring. The rest of the world is out there, getting on with its lives. I am beached in another country, one which I have no optimism of ever being able to leave.

I recollect seeing an old school friend coming towards me on a street in Sheffield, seeing me and crossing to the other side. 'It's because she doesn't know what to say,' I tell myself. But I feel even worse when I realise that we are so tainted by talk of a suicide in the family that people cannot even mumble something. I wouldn't even really mind what they said. Although when another friend said 'I never thought he had the guts to do it', it stung like a slap.

My cousin Ricky comes towards me. Younger than me, six months older than David, Rick spanned the time between us and we three would often spend our weekends together when we were all little at Grannie and Grandpa's red brick farmhouse, Palace Farm, in

Scrooby. This was before Ricky's little sister Sue was born, seven years after Ricky, after which David spent more of these weekends at Nana's flat. David and Ricky would chatter and giggle at night in the double bed while I tried to get to sleep in the single one, next to the window by the pear tree. He was a terror as a tot but he is such comfort to me now, enfolding me in an understanding bear hug.

'I'm so sorry. You don't deserve this. No bloody body does. But come on now, it'll be all right. Eventually,' he says gruffly, with a strong Yorkshire accent. Will it ever be 'all right'? But this genuine human connection is a wisdom which beats anything else. I don't know how long I hold on to him for, probably a few seconds. Maybe I can do this.

St Marwenne's Church, Marhamchurch

We stand as the hearse arrives with my brother's body. His friends, the ones who have been able to come, mostly all around twenty years old, assemble by the kissing-gate at the churchyard entrance. There is a painted wooden sign hung up by the gate, which reads in black script:

> *The place whereon thou standest is holy ground*
> *Do no injury to shrub or flower*
> *For they are dedicated to GOD*
> *And to the memory of the departed*
> *Around thee sleep the dead. Thou too must die.*
> *Consider the end and thou shalt never do amiss.*

Nick, Mike, Simon and Jimmy will share the task of carrying their dead friend. Simon's father asked them to come to their house before-hand and he's given them stiff shots of spirits, for courage. Together they bend their knees, hold their breath, check in with each another and, with one heave, pick up then settle the wooden coffin on the yokes of their shoulders.

David was a bodybuilder for his last seven years, lifting weights, doing hundreds of press-ups, to transform a relatively slight boy's body (once mistaken for my sister when we were riding together) into a Yorkshire version of what a man should look like. These young men, who have shown up for their dead friend in his last minutes above ground, shoulder every push-up, every weight-strained muscle, the physical and emotional struggle now visible in their faces.

They walk in unison, like soldiers, gently delivering their cargo to sit in the middle of the church under the pink and blue-painted renaissance angels. I have looked up at those angels ever since I was five; sometimes they were the last thing I saw before I fainted in church. I was always fainting in church: we weren't allowed breakfast until after communion.

My father speaks. The vicar, Jem, speaks. Perhaps I speak; I don't remember if I did. We probably sing some hymns and say some prayers in the wind-free respite inside St Marwenne's church, before being back in the storm. It is about a hundred yards from the church porch to the side of the grave, enough for whatever dryness is in our clothes to become sodden. The deep grave already holds several inches of muddy water.

Ropes overlie the space in the ground, ribboning in the wind, on top of the wooden planks. My brother-loaded coffin is placed on top by his friends; dropping wood onto wood, exchanging holding up the coffin for holding on to the ropes underneath. As they hold the ropes steady, the planks are pulled away by the undertaker. My brother is lowered by his friends into this cold womb under the horse chestnut tree, bent backwards on this wind-pounded North Cornish coast, to overlook the sea a couple of miles away.

Jem says something else. We each can throw earth on top of the coffin. As I throw mine, I want to throw myself in too. I see my mother, desperately impelled towards what is left of her son. She has to be wrenched away by my father, and he directs her back towards the Salt Box, holding her up under her bent arm. And then that part is done.

'Please do come back and join us at the house, you would be most welcome,' my father repeatedly asks the mourners. The family will come. My brother's friends, too. And others who have known us, or whose politeness (or maybe curiosity, I don't care) includes them. Some people trudge singly or in twos or threes towards the Salt Box.

The fact of a loved one's suicide implies judgement. You were not good enough to hold me. You did not love me well enough, or understand me as I needed. You did not meet my needs. You did not connect with me so my loneliness receded. You fell short.

We can hardly bear to look each other in the face. To stay sane, our task is to hand fairly and squarely the responsibility of choosing life or death back to the person who has taken his life, absolve ourselves of blame. It is not our fault, ultimately it is his responsibility. Blame, guilt, cannot, must not, be contained within us as they will sap and wither our own lives and mean we only live half-lives, or we cannot even continue on earth and we too may die. I don't know this yet.

The hall was painted a few years ago, with foresight, in grey. People take off their wet coats before they move into the dining room, within which the tables have been laid out with the then-standard Yorkshire funeral fare. Ham sandwiches, sausage rolls, slices of pork pie, sausages on sticks (a lot of pigs have died for this meal), vol-au-vents, cheese on sticks, crisps. My father is keen to offer drinks to anyone who will take one. Aunty Judy offers tea or coffee. The latter is probably a safer bet, but I have first one, then more sherries. The third finally brings back some feeling.

'We are so sorry.' 'So sorry. David was a wonderful young man.' 'I'm so sorry. He had his whole life ahead of him.' 'We are terribly sad.' 'What a sad day.' Shrouded, my mother sits in her chair, not speaking much, looking at the carpet. My father starts telling stories about David, how they used to go together to see Doncaster Rovers as well as Sheffield Wednesday, about David playing cricket, and them going to the beach together. Tales of a father and son relationship; a retelling of family life which becomes more and more distant from my own memories. I want to run away.

•

'Anyone seen Nick Cain recently?' asks Simon. I look around and shake my head.

'Not me.'

'No.'

'No, not seen him since the service,' says Mike.

'He said he'd come back here, after,' another friend says.

'But he was, like, wild.' Another friend struggles to find what to say, though uses the adjective most people seem to use when they talk about him.

I'd only seen Nick Cain once, at the Bullers Arms, when he met up with my brother and I was there at the same time. He didn't see me. David's face lit up when he saw his best friend and the two went over to each other – not hugging, but smiling, laughing, hitting one another on the shoulder.

David was tall, dark ginger, with what we in the family called a 'poncho' moustache as it looked Mexican. He resembled a young Ian Botham: 'Beefy', and was still handsome, despite losing his hair. Nick was a bit taller, blond, green-eyed. David wore surfers' bracelets, strips of leather with beads around his wrists, and another beaded thong of leather around his neck. Nick had a single silver chain circling his tanned neck. They were around the same age, Nick a bit younger. His family have a farm nearby, rearing sheep for generations, David told me later. To my A-level Eng Lit eyes, Nick was a mix of Gabriel Oak from Thomas Hardy's *Far from the Madding Crowd* and Heathcliff from Emily Brontë's *Wuthering Heights*. What is it about a man that draws the gaze? He wasn't the most good looking. He had wide-apart green eyes; they smiled as well as his mouth, which was full and dark red. He had a chipped tooth. He was maybe not quite six foot, with strong, working hands and broad shoulders, the result of heaving fencing, lambs and stones around, I later supposed. He was beautiful. While I took all that in I also knew that, as David's best friend, Nick was strictly taboo.

No one has seen him for what must be more than an hour. Since David was laid in the ground. It feels longer; time is dragging. There is still some light in the sky, darkened by the outside storm.

Mike, the keenest, says, 'I'll go and take a look for him. Wouldn't want him to be out in this for long.' He goes, and returns twenty-five minutes later, shaking rain off his hair. 'No sign.'

'Is the Bullers open yet?' asks Simon, the one who usually has a huge smile on his face, though not today.

'No. Pub's shut. Not open for a couple of hours or so.'

'Where've you looked?' I question.

'All round, by his car, the church, down round Under Lane. His car's still there. Tried down everywhere I could think of. No sign. I went home, called his sister. He's not home.' Mike speaks quickly.

They exchange worried looks.

'Maybe he's gone for a walk?' I say.

'He was really, y'know, when he left the church, like, down. He said he wanted to be on his own. He was crying.' More looks are exchanged, in between looking at the floor.

'I'll go,' I decide. 'I've got an idea where he might be.'

'Don't you want anyone to come with you? I'll come,' says Mike.

'No, I'll be OK.' I'm desperate to get out of the house.

I go into the frozen living room.

'I'm going out for a bit,' I say to my mother, quietly. She barely looks up. I glance at my father, say nothing and leave.

It is almost impossible not to bang the door shut when you leave: there is a flailing, light, mock-brass knocker which always knocks whenever the door opens or closes, or even if the wind is up. I step outside, noticing the box hedge by the door needs a trim. I breathe in lungfuls of air as if I'd been holding my breath before.

The rain is still falling as I walk down the tarmacked road to a lane which will lead down to the Bude Canal. Maybe here? I walk down the cobbled grassy path, bigger than a footpath, smaller than a road, overhung on one side with branches of bent-back trees.

No sign. I retrace my steps back towards the centre of the village and breathe again, this time deeper, trying to get my brain working.

Where would I go if I wanted to be alone?

As I come back towards the old village school, I peel off to the left to walk down to the school field, or the Revel Field as it was called, in honour of the Marhamchurch Revel which takes place every year on the second Monday in August. A young girl, a maiden, is chosen from all the girls in the village to be the Revel Queen; to be crowned by Old Father Time, then mount onto a surprisingly steady white horse, ride around the village, and open the village fair on the Revel Field.

Today the weather alone is enough to hide anyone.

On the left of the Revel Field, which slopes out towards Bude, overlooking the sea, is a rough, corrugated iron shed, with round wooden struts and beams and a concrete floor. You can hide here because there is another shed just next to it with solid wooden walls. The big shed is witness to Marhamchurch schoolkids taking their first drag of a cigarette and trying not to be sick, or taking that first tentative kiss when noses and glasses get in the way, and do you turn your face left or right? It is a place of initiation, though by us it was simply called 'Down Revel Field'.

Once you hid at the back of the shed, grown-ups couldn't see you, although you could watch for them if you had to. The shed hasn't changed much in the years since I last hid here. He must be here. But I see no one; no sign, at first. I wait, wondering where to go next. Then I just catch a sort of a primal noise and creep towards it. It is coming from near the low wall at the back of the big shed.

I hear what sounds like, 'No, please, no.' The voice is thick with grief. I edge closer.

'Please God, no. I didn't know you'd do it. Why did you fucking do it?' Nick is talking to himself, crouching on the ground, sobs

The shed at the Revel Field

bursting out of him, like an animal wounded. The desperation in his face scares me and I gasp inadvertently. Nick hears and starts, looking towards the sound.

He startles as he sees me; a stag about to bound away. He jumps to his feet, wiping his face with his hand.

'Helen, is it? What … are you doing here? Are you all right?'

'I came to see if I could find you. People are worried, Nick.'

'I'm … You don't want to be here. Just go away, please, keep me away from you.' He turns his back and starts moving away from the Revel Field towards the river, now full of storm water, rushing down the valley into the Bude Canal.

'Don't go, Nick,' I say, following him. 'Stay. Could we talk a bit? Please?'

I bargain with God. 'Let him talk to me, that's all. That's not much to ask, is it? I won't drink for a week. I'll talk more to my dad. Please God just let him tell me what's going on,' I silently offer up. I need to know Nick will be OK. He was close to my brother.

Nick turns back towards me and I stretch out my hand to grab his wrist. It touches a small gash, scabbed over now. If he moves away now I will hang on to his wrist, though he could bat me off and he'd be faster than me if he runs.

Being close to him, my body changes. This man is strong, with a force around him; not tamed, raw. 'He's wild, that one' echoes around him, but whether he's heard it or not it wouldn't matter. He's there in his own skin, present; he locks your eyes. Like a sea wave crashing, losing balance, when you're in the sea, bubbles, rushing sounds all around and you don't know whether you're up or down until some part of your body brushes sand, scrapes against a rock and you start to orient yourself towards the light, thrusting towards where the sea is brighter, nature taking over.

He pushes me away and heads off, loping into a run. He will leave me too. I lurch after him before he has a chance to build speed and grab an arm. He holds still, then turns around to look at me.

'Look, Nick, you can't go. I'm sorry, please stay, let's talk.' I say over and over. Then, 'Were you there when it happened?' I can't not ask what I'm thinking.

He pulls back. 'No! How could you? Who the hell are you to ask me that?'

I don't answer straight away. The flash dies. 'Sorry,' I say. His face is blotched with crying, and the sobs are coming back.

Then, 'Why do you think you can help me?' he says.

'It's OK, it'll be OK. Let's just talk. It's just terrible now. I'm sorry. You'll get through this. I know it hurts.' I say things like this, that I hope make some kind of sense, though everything is senseless. He says back things like, 'I know. God it must have been a shock for you. This is worse than I could have imagined. It hurts so bad. You'll be all right.'

We start to right ourselves, the breathing coming easier. I still need to know more.

'Is there anything you're not saying? David would want you to tell me.' I say this with a certainty I don't feel, but saying it steadies me and becomes almost factual.

He throws his coat down on the ground. I take off my coat and hold it over us as we sit down, our bodies close, on the wet earth, the rain still falling. We talk.

'I don't know. Can I tell you this? Would you tell anyone else?' he asks. I shake my head, crossing the fingers of my free hand behind my back.

He talks almost as if to himself. 'No one else knew me like he did. He was always laughing, extreme, right? A bit like me. But solid. You knew where you were with him. If we were in a war, we'd have got each other through. He would have my back, I'd have his.

'It was a week or so back, back before, when he died, we'd gone out.' He sounds hollow. 'It was just a … night, see. We were out drinking, the Bullers first, then the Manor. He told me, David told me, about his Dad, your Dad, and how he couldn't do anything right and how he made him hate himself. I knew what he felt, I didn't get on with my dad either and we talked about it. But we were stuck.' Nick's dark mouth tightens.

'And he told me he loved me. We were, like, brothers, see? And then later, on that night …'

I look down at his wrist. Did he cut himself at the farm? Are there drops of my brother's blood mingled in Nick Cain's body? What else happened? Was there a pact to end these precious lives? My mind races but I don't ask any questions; I daren't break this spell. I wait, ache, in silence and take his hand.

'There was this other thing he said,' Nick says, after a while. 'David said, if things won't ever change, then what's the point? He talked about killing himself. I did a bit too, I wish I couldn't say that. And Helen, I promise you I never thought he'd do it. But he has, and … I'm scared, Helen. I can't stop …'

Nick looks at me. We both can't not know anymore. I feel a pang of loyalty.

'We don't know what happened the night he died, Nick, we weren't there. My dad thinks there was an accident. I don't know. Could be. Maybe he got drunk, there were lots of empty bottles, he must have been drunk, maybe he was thinking he might or not and then it just went off …' I am not convincing even myself.

I draw away to search his face but he turns his head down, to gaze into the mud, lost inside.

A yearning for life to carry on lights up, then catches fire in him and me. Tentatively, we tilt in to each other, lips searching to connect amidst the tears and dripping wet hair. For several seconds, I don't know where he begins and I end. God, where is this going?

I pull back and look again at his wrist, stroke it with my thumb. I try to heal him with the warmth of my hand. He turns, looks into my eyes.

'I want you,' he says. 'But that's wrong, isn't it?'

'No,' I reply. 'It's life, being alive. What else matters?'

I uncross my cramped fingers from my hand behind my back and reach both hands to enfold his face in a kiss.

In what right world could loving him ever be a wrong thing to do?

Chapter 14

April 1981, Northcote Farm

'So, you're up now are you?'

'Morning, Father. Or as the Irish say, top of the morning to you.'

'Some bloody top. Half the day's gone. You're missing out on your life, boy.'

'Don't start, Dad. We haven't had a minute.' Nick pours out a big mug of tea, thinking, he doesn't even remember that my best friend has died.

'Will you go down to willow field today? That ewe expecting twins, she weren't looking too good two days back, a bit rakey. Did you check on her yesterday? And take some feed up.'

'Hay'll do it. I'll take up some hay and then see what else has to be done.'

'Get prepared, boy. Take up the feed as well and then you'll be polishing off two jobs at once. Think ahead.'

'If you start getting me on that, what are we planning to do about the bridge then, father? We can't stay like this, we've got to invest, get on with developing this land. And that bridge'll be down before we know it.'

'It's not down to us, it's the estate should sort that out. That bridge has been up for over an 'undred years, it's not going to fall down now.'

'Have you had a look at it in the last few days? The cutwater's high and it looks as if the trusses on the right will be down if we get flooding.'

'We'll put a bit of cement on it for now. I'll give you an 'and if you want to do that. No immediate danger of flooding, is there? Get that ewe sorted this morning. She's worth a bit, that ewe is, even with the prices for lambs we're getting now. Hardly makes it worth it. What with the government and all. If it wasn't for you, for handing it down to you and the grandchildren in future …' he tails off, then orders, 'Take the quad.'

'I was going to anyway, what do you think I am, stupid or something?'

'Well, you shouldn't be, not with me sending you away to school and everything. I've invested in you, you know. And take Kip.'

'And that, too.'

Nick gives a low whistle and Kip – whose eyes are watching father and son, waiting for a command, any hint, to do what pleases him most, which is to please them – responds. Kip especially loves mornings, when the whole day stretches out ahead.

Nick pulls open the heavy oak-framed door, the door which has kept its occupants safe since the 1500s. It's probably the same bleddy door as they had then.

He strides over to the back barn where the quad is parked, then heaves two bales of hay into the back plus a bag of sheep pellets. Kip jumps in almost before he gives the command. He's a bleddy mind reader, Nick thinks, not for the first time.

The dog surveys his domain sideways then turns back round to watch his master. He can't stop himself from leaning in against him, loving his warmth and smell as he does.

'Get back there you bugger, you'll tip out if you try that on the road.' Nick has a flash of embarrassment talking to him, although Kip is his only witness.

Igniting the quad, they snarl down the track, grey granite walls marking out the route to willow field. It's still wet, and the streams nearly overflow as they rush to offload into the big River Tamar. Stone-walled hedges chant 'spring'. Primroses, sweet flashes of light yellow, uncoil in the grass whose winter brown has almost vanished, replaced by the bright lime of new growth. Hazel leaves unfurl like green rain splashes. Dull catkins, duty done to fanfare the season's onset, are now eclipsed by bursts of violets, daffodils, cowslips. Spikes poking up promise bluebells. Despite himself, and this ache now constantly inside, Nick feels alive.

He quickly reaches nearby willow field, one of the most sheltered at the farm, a good one for the early lambing. The ewes are settled here but they are pushing each other around by the wooden five-bar gate: he's a bit later than he should be. He grabs one hay bale, chucks it on the stone wall by the gate, then puts his hands on the top of the gate to swing his body up and over. There's such pleasure to be had from gate leaping. He wonders how many years it will be before it stops being easy, and he'll open and close the gate laboriously, like his father has since forever.

As he cuts the orange twine with his penknife, balling it up in his pocket to put in the quad later, he tears out thick slices of haybale to pitch around the field, so the sheep have space enough to eat without trampling one another. The sheep are counted, then he counts again. One missing. It's the ewe expecting twins who, nearly seven years old, already has five breeding seasons behind her. She's one of the awkward ones, although when Nick is feeling worst off about sheep, he thinks that they're all bloody awkward, there's not an easy bugger amongst them.

'They all want to die, that's their big plan, see.'

He observes each of the sheep, looking out for any problems, judging by sight, sound and smell. Checking if any are grazing on their knees – the cost of getting a vet out to fix a dodgy foot is not worth it, the margins are tight on the sale of lambs, but he hates to see any animal hurting and he calls the vet if he can't sort it out himself.

He's had to make himself wise-hard to be able to kill an animal in pain if there is no other option. If a lamb is born with two heads, or no brain, he's killed it without blinking. Life – good life – needs to be treasured and succoured. When life cannot thrive, it's best to make an early decision.

The health of the overall flock is his focus. If a sheep is in distress, she might maa a warning, until she gives up hope, her eyes glaze over and she starts the panting surrender into death. The smell of a dead sheep will also be a sign that Nick looks out for, however unwelcome. He monitors the weather, the temperature, how much humidity is in the air, if it looks like a storm is coming. The worst of the winter is over and these sheep will be out in the fields until the next, but a deep frost or snow could still bring problems. Nick has to work with, not against, the weather. He never talks about his job with his friends. It means too much to him as well as nothing at all. He worries that the sheep will become his life and he'll have no chance to see the opposite side of the world, Australia. That in future he won't turn beyond page four of the map book, like other locals, although he's been away to school and that gave him another view. And then there's David. Don't think about that now. You can talk to Helen later.

He looks around the field, listening intently for a cry of distress, anything really that will give him a clue about what's going on. The only alarm is a blackbird squawking, but that'll be because Kip's around. He smells the air, sweeping the field from front to back. Nothing, but there's still the dip at the back of the field leading to the stream, the part you can't see, with the old rusted gate which he should've fixed before.

He walks over to this farthest edge, hearing the maa-ing of the flock get fainter as he heads up and down over the ridge. At first he can't see her, she's chosen the worst place of all, right in the brambles. He goes over to inspect. It'll be hard getting the quad up and over here, he might even have to drag her body up, heavy not only from the weight of her twins but also the wet. Her eyes are wide open, staring. Bastards. It's all sheep ever want to do, die, I bet she woke up thinking about it. Well, she's got her wish now. It's her revenge. We take her children away: this is what she does to get back at us.

He almost respects her for it, before he remembers what a literal drag it will be. And yet another thing for his father to blame on him. And then he lets himself think of his best friend. His mind always rests on him first.

Chapter 15

Monica

I can't bear this. I'm going to have to stay at home, for ever, with Geoffrey conducting Mozart on the gramophone and crying. It makes me ill. He doesn't ask me what I'm feeling. Nor do I do ask him. We don't ask questions: we don't want to know the answers.

I was the apple of my daddy's eye, that's why I was called Pip, but you know that of course. And you were the apple of my eye. My little treasure. You were my blue-eyed angel. I idolised you. Your blond hair, almost white when you were very little. Soft curls. I used to tease those curls to make them curlier. Those were the best days. When you got older, when you started to become a man, your hair grew straight, darker, a bit gingery like Geoffrey's, and your face got stubbly. I didn't like that.

Then when you were twenty your hair fell out. Such bad luck. They say it depends on the maternal grandfather how long you keep your hair, but I don't really know. I never went to Uni-ver-si-ty, it was my mother who stopped me from doing all of that. She made me go out to work and get married, not University. I didn't like my mother, although I don't say that out loud.

You and me were more like my father, like Les, everyone could see that. His mother, my father, me, my son – you, David – we were all alike. Blond hair, blue eyes, quieter. We didn't say much, we didn't need to. We were more practical. You always were taking things apart, putting them back together again. We kept ourselves to ourselves, that was our way.

It cost me a lot to have you: maybe you don't know that because I didn't tell you, or anyone really, apart from Gwen. I never let on, because I had you and that made it all alright. My mother even said, 'Well done, Pip.' That was the first time I think she ever said that.

Though I remember Helen's birth: good God, that pain. I said to the matron, I'm far too tired to have this baby now. Put me to sleep. I will have the baby tomorrow but *not* today. She looked me in the eye and she knew I wouldn't be crossed. So she gave me something, and I went to sleep. And then I had to go through it all again the following day. I thought it might have happened overnight, while I was asleep. At least then Helen was born on the same day as the Queen, not Hitler. April 21st is the Queen's proper birthday, not her official one in June, which is more for the tourists. But her birth tore me. I had to be sewn back up, nice and tidy, ready for my husband, the marital duty. Only six weeks of peace and quiet.

I have a rare blood group. I'm B rhesus negative; Geoffrey is B rhesus positive. The doctors said that our first child would be born satisfactorily, any second baby would have difficulties, and then we mustn't have any more, because they wouldn't survive. My blood would attack the baby in the womb because it would be foreign.

My first baby was fine. And then you were too, such a bonny babe. Your birth was easier, I knew what I had to go through to be a mother, I didn't put it off again.

But Geoffrey thought we should try to have another baby, just to see, it wouldn't hurt to try would it? But it didn't work out. I lost that baby. My body couldn't hold on to it.

And I now couldn't hold on to you. I've lost you because of what you did. Although that's another thing I don't openly say, never in front of Geoffrey. It would kill him.

Behind every great man there's a great woman, they say. Geoffrey needed me. People noticed that, although not those people at the Law Society. They did not see who it was who made things happen. Anyway, I preferred to have a nice sit down, to be at the back.

But we had a grand life, so many interesting people, places, wonderful parties. I organised them. We went to the Queen's garden party twice in a row. Geoffrey always said it was because he was President of the Yorkshire Union of Law Societies for all those decades. Nonsense. It was because I was a Guide Commissioner and did all those good works.

I don't really like other people. I would say, 'I don't like animals. Or babies. Apart from my own, of course.' I always had to remember myself and say those last six words. People would look at me in shock, as if there was something wrong with me. But I knew things other people didn't. I was so close to Helen I could feel if she was having a headache. I have always been different, God made me that way.

Geoffrey and I have never talked about that other side of me. He didn't want to know. He didn't talk to me when he was cross, either. It only started after we married, when we had our first and only row, and it was all about the wallpaper. He never knew what he was doing about practical matters. We didn't talk for ten days after that. Later on, if I got my hair cut short, like I like it, he wouldn't talk for four days. He wanted my hair long, either curling down my back or up in a bun, at the top of my head. He said I was beautiful that way.

Sometimes it takes a lifetime to work out problems in a relationship. It's best not to talk about things that won't change. Geoffrey and I have an agreement about that. What is the point of talking about something that stays the same? People are always wanting to talk about things, talk, talk, chatter, chatter. I say things if they need saying. But if in doubt, don't say anything. I don't give myself away.

The drinking will help, once I can drink again, when we come to terms with what's happened like Geoffrey says. When we're in company, I expect that Geoffrey will say to me, 'Monica, you're tired. It's time for you to go to bed,' like he did before and I will do what he says. I have to admit, I do feel tired. We have rules. It makes for a quieter life. We will get by, get there. What's the alternative?

Chapter 16

April 1981

A couple of weeks later I am back again at the Salt Box, my parents having now returned to Doncaster to sort things out there. I promised I would help tidy the garden up, plant some peas, walk Cleo.

My dad said, 'It would be good for you to have a break.'

Whenever I can, I am with Nick.

When I first saw him naked his torso was chalk white, stark in contrast to his dark gold face, neck and arms. Our lovemaking is intense. One or other of us often cries, or both, and there is so much pain still around, it's too hard to sift through which feeling means what.

One morning, lying in bed watching the sun come up, I feel a hopeful wave run through me; something different, even though the blackness still waits in the corner. An unthinking 'I love you' blurts out.

Then quickly afterwards, 'I didn't mean to say that. Well, I mean, I didn't mean to say it out loud. I'm sorry.'

'Do you feel it, Helen? Is that true?' No point in trying to twist away.

'Yes.'

Nick throws himself on his back on the bed, his chain and blond strands of hair falling back on the pillow. He looks up at the ceiling, eyes wide open, quite still. I say nothing.

'Oh God,' he says, on a light outbreath.

'What's wrong?'

'I do too. I love you!' He says it amazedly, as if in shock. 'I love you.' Laughing, he jumps up out of bed and dances around the room, a sheet half covering him. 'I love you, Helen.'

'Well, that's that then,' he says, before pulling me towards him.

•

Nick left at about midnight, neither of us wanting to part but he had to be up early the following morning for work on the farm. I wasn't sleeping well, although I hadn't for years anyway, I had never got the habit then. At around 7.25 a.m. the bakelite phone rang downstairs in the living room, its insistent double trill, then a bit of a gap, then twice more, then a gap. It wasn't going away. I didn't want to get up. Bed always seemed a safer place than anywhere else. I crawled downstairs, the phone ringing all the time.

'Widemouth Bay 213?' I answered.

'Is that Helen? It's Nick Cain's sister here.'

Everyone seemed to call him by both names, even his sister. Maybe because they were both a single syllable.

'Is he with you? He's not at the farm. Have you heard from him? I thought he might've called you.'

'No, haven't heard from him today yet, sorry.'

'By the way, I'm very sorry about your brother. Awful. So young. It's affected Nick.'

'What's happened?'

'It's his car, Nick's car's been found, rolled over in a ditch, it's near the Coach and Horses. Someone reported it to the police and they called us. He's not there. The police are trying to find him now. My parents are so worried.'

An accident? The police? Oh God.

'Whereabouts? Was there any blood, I mean, sorry, I really don't know why I said that, what do the police think happened? Was there anyone else involved?' Only two questions mattered. Where the hell was he? Was he OK?

'This must be terrible for you.' I said. I couldn't say, I'm sure it will be all right.

'The windscreen's cracked. His car might be a write-off, don't know yet, but it doesn't look like any other vehicle was involved.'

'Is there anything I can do to help? Can I help search for him?'

'It's best if you stay by your phone, he'll maybe call you. He won't come back home, that's what I think. His dad is more worried about him than anything else. We want to know he's OK. That's all.'

'Can you give me your number? I'll call you if I hear anything. But I want to come out and search.'

Jotting her telephone number down, I looked at the grandfather clock. 7.32 a.m. Another day without David. And now Nick?

•

Two hours later, the phone rings, persistently. Brrrp, Brrrp, pause. Brrp, Brrp, pause. I let it ring, frozen, for five rounds. I don't want to answer if it's bad news. I pick up.

'Helen?' It's him.

'Yes, it is. Oh, thank God. Your sister called. You OK? Tell me you're all right.'

'I'm calling you from a phone box, I'm like OK, a couple of bruises like, but nothing broken, as far as I can tell. I didn't know what to do. I've been walking around, for hours, it's kept me warm. It's my dad I've been thinking about, what's he going to do? He'll be mad as hell at me for this stunt.'

'Your sister said not to worry. He just wants to know you're all right. Everyone does. I couldn't stand it if. Shall I come and pick you up?'

'Proper job. Then we can go back to yours.'

'We should go back and face your dad.'

'No, Helen, not that.'

'Well, let me come and get you and we can talk about it. Where are you?'

Nick gives me a spot miles from anywhere I know.

'I'll look it up on the map. Be there in, I dunno, twenty minutes? Don't go anywhere else. Don't move.'

'OK then. Love you.'

We say that as if it's not a big thing. We avoid the g-word though: farewells are harder.

I drive, reminding myself as I swing round a corner too fast that I won't be doing anyone any good if I total my car too. I force myself consciously to slow down. If one tragedy happens, others come in its wake. It's contagious, like all emotions.

Nick's sitting on an old tumbling-down grey stone wall, by a stile, in a layby at the side of the road, hunched against the cold, his eyebrows creased.

'He's going to kill me, Helen.'

'He needs you on the farm. So that's not going to happen.'

'But he'll be bleddy mad with me. I'd be bleddy mad with me if I was him.'

'How about if I go in first, draw the fire.'

'You sure? I'm not sure my mother will be up to a visit from you yet.'

'She'll be relieved to see you and she'll just have to put up with seeing me.'

We draw nearer where he lives; it's first time I've seen it. North-cote is a tiny hamlet, with only half the number of people who lived there a hundred years ago. We walk under an arch to get to the farm, dark gold Devonian stone.

A collie by the door barks once. Maybe it would have barked more if Nick were not there.

His mother brings out a pot of tea and homemade biscuits, set out on a pretty floral plate with a gilt edge, and places them on the large, scrubbed, wooden farm table. She wears a well-washed apron, with a blouse and skirt underneath.

His father leaves it to her to offer tea, pour out and proffer the cup and saucer to each of us. 'Do you take sugar?' she asks.

'So what have you done this time, boy?' Nick's father turns to him. He looks more like Nick Cain's grandfather than his father.

'He didn't mean to, Mr Cain, it was an accident. He is really sorry, I know it, he's been saying it all the way in the car,' I yabber.

'I want to hear it from him.'

Nick takes longer to reply. I can see his jaw clenched.

'I'm sorry, father. It was an accident.'

'Well you'd better get it sorted. Had you been drinking then?'

'I will sort it. And I wasn't drinking.'

This was true. Nick and I exchange glances, 'Helen's got to get off now, Dad, Mum. I'm just going to go back with her to her car.'

I say an awkward goodbye and we head back to my Renault.

'Are you going to be OK?'

'Sure. I'll call you, when the storm's passed.'

Chapter 17

I loved Nick Cain, no doubt. I loved him enough to set him free if that's what he wanted. Like if a butterfly were to land on your open hand. Don't close your hand up, you'll kill it. Keep your palm open and see what happens.

I needed him to live, that went without saying. We did not manage to spend as much time together as we'd hoped but sometimes I was able to get away to the Salt Box, when my parents weren't there, and one weekend we even went to Derbyshire and Yorkshire, visiting places important to my brother and me. Above all, we needed space.

'I hate being on the farm, Helen. I love the land and all that but between my dad and me, there's … I feel trapped.'

'What is it you want, what do you dream about?' I asked, across the table. 'What's the most important thing for you?'

I hoped he'd say he wanted me. I wanted to be enough; to be the solution. He paused and hesitated before turning his head to look at me sideways, opening his mouth to a smile.

'I don't know if I can tell you this, Helen. I don't know how you'll take it.'

'Try me.'

'It might hurt you.'

'I said try me, didn't I?'

'Oh, but what's the point in even thinking it? There's so much I could do, cities to visit. Maybe Las Vegas, I should go there. That would be a right laugh. David would piss himself if he thought I was going to Las Vegas.' We both giggled. It was absurd.

'But if that's what you want, go for it. If you try it and you hate it, at least you can cross that one off your list.'

'No, that's not it. I don't think I know what I want. I love the farm, even the sheep, well when they're not trying to bleddy kill themselves, but I don't know if it's enough. It's my dad, see? I keep thinking about what I should do.'

'OK. Let's not focus on what you don't want. Here …'

I threw him a notepad and a pen.

'What do you want? Write that down. I dunno – make a list.'

'I don't bleddy know.' He threw the notepad and pen back on the table. 'We're going round in circles, I've told you already. It's not as simple as that. There's responsibilities I've got. You can't just say to sheep "I'm off to meet my destiny".'

'OK, let's try something else. Write down, "Things I am sure about" and then start.'

'OK.' He concentrated, pen on paper.

'I am sure … that I love Helen.' He looked over at me and smiled, then looked straight into my eyes. My heart leaped, although even as he looked at me I didn't believe what he was saying.

'I am sure that I love a drink.'

'Oh, yeah, that.'

'I am sure that David was my best mate ever.'

He broke off, throwing the pen back down on the table. He was one of the few men I ever met who was secure and confident enough in himself to cry. Between us, we had cried a lot.

He had written only one word on the page. 'David'.

I hugged him. 'Is this not helping?'

'OK, then, I will tell you. There're two things. I want to go to Australia, Helen, always have, ever since I was a boy. Big country, big sheep country, must be enormous skies. It'd be hot, Bondi Beach, all of that, you know.' He laughs, and sketches an hourglass shape with his hands. 'It won't happen. It's a dream. But you asked …'

I flinched inside, the prospect of losing him to the other side of the globe hitting home.

'If we're in this together, then we need get good at making dreams come true. We've had enough of a nightmare to last anyone's lifetime. What's stopping you?'

'Apart from you, you mean?'

'Come on, that's not fair.'

'It's my dad, mainly. I'm needed on the farm. He can't run it on his own and we can't get in anyone else, he'd say we can't afford it. He'd say, "Bugger me, boy, why do ee want to do that?" It's not going to happen. No way. I shouldn't even think about it.'

'Should, shouldn't, must, mustn't, ought, oughtn't. Stop. They don't get you anywhere. "If" is better. If you, if we, could find you a way to go to Australia. Why not? If you don't take your chance now, you'll be retired – or dead – before you do it. You need to live your dreams, that's why you have them. It's your soul beckoning you.'

He really laughed then. 'You're bleddy mad, Helen, do you know that?'

'So it's not mad to live and die on the farm and never give yourself a chance in life, to experience anything else, go out into the world, is that what you're saying? Give it a go. I'll come over to see your Dad with you.'

'Why would you do that? He'll never agree anyway.'

'If he doesn't, you could just walk.'

'Where would I go?'

'You could come and live with me for a bit.'

'In London? Good God, I'd die. What would I do there? Mike said if I went there the only thing I could do would be to give old men blow jobs at a tenner a shot.'

I looked at him, shocked. 'Listen, I just want you to be happy.'

'Come here. I know a way you can make me happy.'

I pushed him away. 'Think about it. I bet you can do this. How hard can it be? You're an adult. He can't stop you. You might think it's a problem, but it won't be unless you think it. Get practical. When is it best for you to go? And how are you going to pay for it?'

'I've got money saved up. And my dad might give me a bit more. It's better after the summer, after the lambs have gone to market, but then I'd want to go to Australia for at least six months. Do you really think?'

'Yes. I really think. I'm a bleddy lawyer, ain't I?' (said in an affected West Country accent).

'And what do you want, Helen?'

I told him one thing. To be a partner in a firm in London by the time I'm thirty.

I didn't tell him I wanted to meet Alan Bates (I'd always loved Alan Bates, ever since he was Gabriel Oak in *Far from the Madding Crowd*), get married by the time I was thirty and, most of all, have children. I longed for kids, and my parents had told me if I didn't marry before I was thirty no man would ever want me. There are things you can't say.

He pulled me to him again and stroked my hair, then cupped the back of my head with both hands.

I started to melt, but remembered. 'Hold on a bit. You said there are two things you want to do, two dreams. What's the second dream?'

'Ah, that. I want to learn how to fly.'

Chapter 18

24th April 1981

The first inquest is held at HM Coroner's Office in Nottinghamshire, three days after my birthday, which I don't want to celebrate. My father suggests that I don't come. It should only be a formality. I am relieved not to have to go and listen to my father giving evidence. That, in particular, I can't imagine being able to do.

The inquest takes place on a Friday, and the coroner has six other cases to deal with. Apart from the Slade Hooton statements, the main statements will be from the pathologist, who will not be called in evidence, the neighbour (a schoolteacher in Bothamsall) and a gun-shop owner from Sheffield. My father will also give evidence to add to the statement he made on the day he found my brother dead, and he will be cross examined. There is a letter from Reverend Jeremy Parsons, the vicar, submitted in evidence too. The court is presided over by coroner Lieutenant Colonel Harry Thompson, a retired army officer although he still uses his title (something my father despises).

This is what the coroner will read and hear: the key evidence on which he will form and announce his verdict.

DCI Hodgson and Dr Penny present at necropsy 11.20 a.m. 2.3.81

NOTTINGHAMSHIRE AREA HEALTH AUTHORITY

(TEACHING) WORKSOP AND RETFORD DISTRICT

Pathology Department

REPORT OF POST-MORTEM EXAMINATION

Lab. Ref   424.3.81

Date   2 March 1981

Name   GARLICK David Nicholas

Age 20   Sex Male

Address   13 Albion Place, Doncaster

Referred by   H.M. Coroner

Relevant History Was found dead on the floor at Bothamsall Hall
with a gunshot wound to the head. Brain tissue was present in an
approximately straight line across the floor, wall and ceiling. The
body was lying on a single-barrelled 12 bore shotgun. The breech
contained a fired 12 bore No. 7 trap cartridge. There was blood
soaking on the floor beneath the head. Rigor mortis was complete
and the body did not appear to have been moved before I saw it at
5.30 p.m., 1 March 1981.

<u>Externally</u> Thin male, approximately 1.75m tall with a
light brown poncho style moustache. There is fragmentation
of the skull, much of the vortex is missing and there are gross
lacerations of the skin. Linear scorch marks present on the thenar
eminence of the left hand and on the palmar surfaces of 1,2,3, and
4 fingers. Early green discolouration of abdomen.

<u>Internally</u> There is pink discolouration of the anterior
pericardial sac. Aorta circumference 42mm. Pallor of the
kidneys and early green discolouration of the lower lobes. A
cyst in the cortex of the left kidney. Patches of green mottling
of the right lower lobe of lung. Drying stomach contents in
the right lower lobe bronchus. The stomach contains partially
digested food residues and some pink powdery material
compatible with the antiseptic lozenges found in the deceased's

pocket. Liver and spleen show early post-mortem autolysis. Two spider naevi in the shock area of the endocardium. A smell of alcohol present. Slight myocardial softening. No cartridge wads detected. A few pellets present compatible with size 7 shot. The brain is disintegrated and mainly lost but the cerebellum is recognisable.

Conclusion: The findings are compatible with the deceased holding the barrel of the shotgun in his left hand and against the centre of his forehead at the time it was fired.

Cause of death: 1(a) Gun-shot wound.

Histological examination of stained sections: Blood for alcohol and carbon monoxide percentage saturation.
Urine for alcohol content.
Histology showed alcohol content 109 mg/100ml

Pathologist: W Parry MD FRC Path
2.3.81

Statement of	Geoffrey Cameron Garlick
Age	Over 21
Occupation	Solicitor
Address	13 Albion Place
	Doncaster
Tel	Home: 20592, Business: 67139

Dated the 1st day of March 1981

states I am a solicitor and I reside at the above address.

I am the father of David Nicholas GARLICK born 31.5.60 at Doncaster.

I am the solicitor and attorney for [████████], the owner of Bothamsall Hall who has been abroad since July 1980. There was an original arrangement whereby a Mr [████████] was to live in the Hall. When this did not materialise, I arranged for my son David to live in the Hall as custodian with his dog. This has been maintained since October 1980 and I and my wife have visited the Hall almost every week since then.

As far as the keys are concerned, David was given a large metal key for the rear door and I have retained a key in my office for the front door.

The last time I saw David alive was on 12th February 1981 when I and my wife visited him for dinner at Bothamsall Hall.

We left about 7.30 p.m. that day, went to London, and then flew to Cyprus.

On 28th February 1981, I attempted [to] telephone David at Bothamsall but there was trouble with the telephone and the operator said there was a fault on the line.

On Sunday 1st March 1981 around 4 p.m., my wife and I visited Bothamsall Hall intending to have a meal with David.

David's Renault car was parked in the normal place and I rang the front door bell as was the usual practice but there was no reply.

I then went to the back door and could see in the lock a key on a bobbin that was unfamiliar to me. The door was closed but not locked. I entered the Hall and made my way into the sitting room where I saw that the lights were on, the television was on and the curtains were closed.

I then saw my son lying on the floor. He had a large head wound and I recognised him to be dead.

I instantly called the police and have identified the body to DCI Hodgson.

I remember seeing that the lights were also on in the kitchen. There was no sign of my son's black and tan Gordon setter dog which answers to the name of Cleo.

As far as I am aware my son has no shotgun or shotgun certificate.

Until June 1980 my son was a student at Portsmouth Polytechnic but withdrew from his course and spent much of the summer living in Cornwall at the family house.

My son was quite used to living on his own.

My son was in good health, had no financial problems and as far as I was aware had no troubles at all.

David was aware that the owner was returning on 10th March 1981 and in anticipation of this had collected his belongings together which I found in the kitchen near the rear door, together with his telescope which he had for a hobby.

I also saw a small black and white bag in the kitchen and my attention was drawn to the fact that there was a shotgun cartridge in the bag.

Statement of	Alfred John Higginbottom
Age	Over 21
Occupation	School Master
Address	[█████████████]
	Church Lane
	Bothamsall
	Retford
	Notts
Tel	[█████████]

Dated the 2nd day of March 1981

    states I am a Schoolmaster and I reside at the above address.

    My bungalow is at the end of Church Lane, Bothamsall, which is a no through road.

    The property adjacent to mine is Bothamsall Hall owned by Mr [████████]

    Sometime last summer, Mr [████████] went away to travel abroad leaving the Hall unoccupied.

    Towards the end of 1980, I realised that someone else was living in the Hall again because of lights being on and a car parked in the drive.

    Approximately three weeks ago I saw a young man standing near the Hall.

    At approximately 2.30 p.m. Saturday 21st February 1981, I was working on my greenhouse in my rear garden when the man whom I had seen near the Hall previously, came walking past me from the Hall in the direction of the fields. At this time I saw the man was exercising a black and tan Gordon setter dog.

    On this occasion no conversation took place between us.

    Approximately ten to fifteen minutes later the man returned across the fields with his dog. As the man walked past me, I passed a comment about the weather and said, 'Good afternoon.'

    The man then stopped and we had a general conversation about the weather before the man continued on towards the Hall.

    The man spoke with a Yorkshire accent. He appeared to be around 25 years of age and had a full gingerish beard but appeared to be balding rather prematurely. I was able to see the top of the man's head because I was working on the top of the greenhouse. I can't remember anything else very clearly because it's only the second time I've ever seen the man.

At this time the man appeared to be in a normal state of mind. He did not seem nervous or upset and appeared to be enjoying his walk.

Over the past two weeks, I have noticed that the kitchen light in the Hall has been left on at all times but other than that I have seen nothing unusual.

Last Tuesday the 24th February 1981, I received a card in my own mail addressed to a Mr Garlick of Bothamsall Hall. The card was from Cyprus and I believe it was sent by Mr Garlick's parents.

The following morning, Wednesday 25th February 1981, I called at the Hall on my way to work.

At this time, I saw no one around. I didn't ring the bell, I simply placed the post card through the letter box but I remember it didn't drop completely through because the corner of the card remained caught in the letter box flap.

I remember seeing the yellow car parked against the kitchen window but I can't remember which way it was facing.

Statement of	Stephen Hill
Age	Over 21
Occupation	Gunsmith
Address	[██████████████]

Dated the 31st day of March 1981

states I am a director of Arthur Turner (Sheffield) Ltd and I reside at the above address.

The above business is a gunsmith and fishing tackle business.

On Saturday 21st March 1981 I was shown a Baikal 12 bore single barrel shotgun bearing the Serial no. C20019 by DC Ashworth.

Upon checking my records, I can state that on 13th February 1981 I purchased this weapon from a Mr [███████████] of [█████████].

The shotgun was put on display for sale and on 20th February 1981 I sold the gun to a man producing shotgun certificate number 14414 issued by the Nottinghamshire Constabulary to Mr [███████████], Bothamsall Hall, Bothamsall, Retford, Notts.

THE PARISH CHURCH OF S. MARWENNE,
MARHAMCHURCH

1st April 1981

Dear Geoffrey and Monica,

Thank you for your letter.

I am glad to confirm what I have told you of my last meeting with David at Marhamchurch in mid February. One evening in the Bullers Arms I had a drink and a conversation lasting about half an hour with David and [Nick Cain], a friend of his. David seemed perfectly fit and contented. I noticed nothing unusual about his manner and he seemed relaxed, happy and carefree as ever. It came as a tremendous shock and surprise to me when I heard of his death. I hope that these comments are of some help.

Please convey my best wishes to Helen as she starts her new job.

Looking forward to seeing you at Easter,

Yours ever,

[Jeremy Parsons]

The following evidence, given at the inquest by my father, is reconstructed from notes taken by the reporter from the Sheffield Star, *who was at the inquest.*

I arranged for my son to look after Bothamsall Hall. He accepted the very serious responsibility. He started his caretaking role in October 1980. I visited regularly and he came to Doncaster to see us, my wife, his mother, and I. I last saw him alive on Thursday 12th February 1981. My wife and I were going on holiday and called at Bothamsall Hall in the evening and had a meal with him. We spent the evening with him and then went on to London and from there on holiday abroad. We came home again on the evening of 27th February and stayed in London that night. I telephoned my son on the Sunday morning but the line was out of order. The faults department at the GPO said they were checking the fault. I called round on Sunday 1st March in the afternoon on the way home from London. His car was there in the usual place in the yard near the door. The door (back) was not locked – the lights were on. There was a key with a bobbin on it I did not recognise. I went into the lounge he had been using as a sitting room. The lights were on, curtains closed and television on. I did not see my son immediately until I got into the room and saw him lying on the floor near the settee. I saw his eyes were open and thought he must have been asleep. Then I saw the wound on his head and realised he was dead. I telephoned the police. There were other lights on in the house in the kitchen area. He did not own a shotgun to my knowledge. He did not have a certificate. He was not familiar with shotguns. We had lived in areas where there was game and shooting was quite normal. He was interested in clay pigeon shooting but did not himself shoot. He was not familiar with shotguns to handle them.

There was a dog there with him – a setter – but it was not there when I arrived. He was quite used to being on his own which was why I was able to ask him to look after the hall. He was in very good health and had no financial problems. He had no troubles and was in remarkably good spirits when we left him. He knew the owner was coming back and he was prepared to leave. All his belongings were neatly collected ready to go in the next few days. I saw what I thought was a poker, which must have been the barrel, sticking out from under the body. I did not realise then it was a gun. My reaction when I saw him and telephoned the police was that someone must have broken in and attacked him. There were cartridges left in the house by the owner but a gun belonging to him was away for repair. There was a small white bag with cartridges in beside my son's body. I am convinced it was nothing other than a tragic accident. Literally he was in good spirits. He was intending to go to Cornwall. I went down there after his death and established he had been there a few days prior to going down. The rector there had formed a cricket team and he had seen David a few days before. He had gone to great pains to get the home we had there ready. He had dug the garden over and was obviously prepared to go there for some days. I found a leaflet with regard to a shotgun among his papers. He was interested in fishing, motorcycles and sport. Bothamsall is the centre of a shooting area.

He knew this was the last week he would have been at the Hall and would have been an opportunity to do some shooting which I as a solicitor and father better not know about. He had no licence. After taking on the heavy responsibilities of guarding an extensive property he possibly decided to exercise the shooting rights in the last few days and I was not to know. He was not familiar with the mechanics of a shotgun.

The following evidence and proceedings have been reproduced from the notes of the Sheffield Star *reporter.*

Stephen Hill (the gunsmith). Identified single barrel 12-bore shotgun (C20019) from records as gun sold to David Garlick. Looked at certificate at point of sale, name was that of [███████]. Subsequently learned the person I sold the gun to was David Garlick. Circumstances were so ordinary I did not really remember anything specific. I presume he came in to buy a modestly priced, single barrel shotgun. One has got to produce a certificate before purchasing and he produced one. It was not in his name but I did not know that at the time. Mr Hill requested permission from the Coroner to demonstrate why, in his opinion, it would have been 'very difficult indeed for him to have shot himself'. This demonstration was given by Mr Hill who referred to the difficulty in aligning the shotgun and reaching the trigger even with his own 'disproportionately long arms'.

Det Chief Insp Ian Hodgson. I found the key in door. Near the settee was the body of a young man later identified as David Garlick. The gun was underneath him and his left hand was in contact with the barrel. He was clearly dead. There was a shotgun wound. I took possession of the shotgun.

It is true to say that in the house there was a large quantity of unspent cartridges of the gun's calibre. There was also a bag in the kitchen containing unspent cartridges identical to the one taken from the gun.

CORONER The post-mortem report states scorch marks showing the gun was discharged very close to the face. Cause of death was shotgun wound, compatible with him having held the barrel with his left hand against his forehead and fired. Described incident as insoluble problem. This young man was killed instantly by this shotgun wound.

The question is whether he bought the gun with the specific intention of taking his life, or, as his father suggests, as he was leaving Bothamsall he may as well have a bit of shooting while he was there and he was certainly not going to let his father know what he was going to do. It is possible he shot himself accidentally while he was trying to make [sure] certain cartridges he found in the house fitted all right, but it sounds unlikely.

The strongest certainty is that undoubtedly for some reason we do not know and never will know, David Garlick deliberately took his own life, in this rather complicated way.

What we do not know is why this happened.

VERDICT – Took life while balance of mind was disturbed.

Chapter 19

Geoffrey

David, my son. My little boy. I love you so very much, my dear little son, you meant the world to me and your mother. And to your sister Helen of course. I remember back when you were just born, I went straightaway to telephone my father from the public call box at the nursing home, he was getting towards his end then, to tell him you had arrived.

'Father,' I said, 'we have a son. His name will be David Nicholas Garlick, we have decided that, Monica and I. David means beloved, that was my choice, and Nicholas means victory of the people, that was Monica's. I wanted you to be the first to know. He weighs eight pounds four ounces. Both mother and son are doing well.'

I was so proud. It was what we would call in Cambridge *a tolerable day*.

You don't remember Bampa do you, David? He died before you ever got to know him. Such a shame. Three generations of Garlicks, of Garlick men, together, we would have been. Once you were born, I had two children too, like your uncle Jimmy. He had his son first and I had a daughter first, but then you were here. And you, my boy, as my son, you were going to go to Cambridge, perhaps my old college, read law, be a chip off the old block. Cambridge, my old college Sidney Sussex, of course, but you should know that, made me who I am today. The punting, hockey, such witty conversation: I dared to believe I could do anything. It would have done you so much good to have gone there. I saw it all. That was what I wanted for you. It wasn't too much, was it? I genuinely thought that it would make you happy; you just needed to reach for those stars and they were there for the picking.

You could have had that life. What a difference that would have made to all of our lives. Hamilton Haigh, your prep school headmaster, said you were clever. You were top of your class, in just about everything, apart from French and Latin. You should have been able to do better there. After all I was a classics scholar at Cambridge and your grandmother went to the Sorbonne just after the First World War.

What happened, David? You had to work later on. But you wouldn't. You were so damn awkward. I kept on asking you, 'Why won't you do your homework? Why don't you do what you're told?' Terribly boring. I had better things to do than having to repeat 'Practise your times tables. Come on, David, put in a bit of effort'. But you'd slip away, go off and play with your bikes, or go fishing or collect your birds' eggs, or whatever other nonsense you had in your head. What a waste of time, wasting your time and my time too.

I had to tell you, you forced me to it, I had no choice, to spell it out to you. 'You're useless. Stupid boy,' I'd say, on occasions. I only said it because I wanted you to do well, can't you understand that? If anyone had called me stupid, I would have worked harder, I would have shown them. It was because I loved you, David. But you didn't seem to want to see that. I didn't know what was wrong with you.

We had our interests in football and in cricket together, we shared that, wasn't that right? And in beer too, although let's not go there, my boy. Do you remember when I would take you to Sheffield Wednesday, to Hillsborough, to watch the match? 'Up the Owls!' we'd cry, and you'd wave your banner and smile. And they used to win matches six–nil, eight–nil, ten–nil, sometimes. Those were the great days, days to remember. Not like now. That was before.

And do you remember how when we went round the new house at Tickhill, Leahurst, when I showed you and Helen around all the rooms downstairs, the living room, the kitchen, the drawing room, the scullery, and then we all went upstairs and I said, 'Look, this will be your bedroom, and this will be Helen's bedroom. Look here, hers overlooks the car and the walnut tree and yours overlooks the orchard. You've got the bigger room. And, come with me, look over here, this will be Mummy and Daddy's bedroom.'

And you surveyed it all and looked at me, straight at me, and said in your clear young voice, 'And when you die Daddy, this will all be mine.' You were only three years old. I dined out on that story many a time.

Didn't quite work out that way did it, my son?

Should I have done something else? Nobody told me what I should have done differently. I put a roof over your head, you were fed, weren't you, and warm? You were to the manor born. You had all the things that I didn't have when I was a boy, all the things that I'd wanted to have. And what else was I supposed to do? You never said you wanted anything else, you never asked me for anything, except for that car. That didn't turn out very well either, but that wasn't my fault.

But I can't think of this now. I think about when the next drink will be, how much I will need to get hold of to, to feel better, to feel numb. And I have to judge how much Monica has had to drink, if she's coping. If she drinks too much, and she very often does, I have to tell her to go to bed. I tell her she is tired and needs to go to bed. She understands that and she does what I say, for once. It is hard for both of us but there's no point in dwelling on that.

I never wanted you to die, David. I could never have even contemplated that this would happen. Do I need to tell you that? I knew we'd been a bit out of touch but not this, David, why? It's the one word which I go to bed with, and wake up to in the morning. It whines around and around my head, even though I will not spend any time deliberately thinking about it. But it won't go away.

It cannot have been you David, how dare they say that, how dare anyone say that? If anyone does, I shoot them a stare. They don't mention it again.

I am quite certain in my own mind that it must have been something else, someone else, anyone else. Perhaps it was an accident, possibly, that's a possibility I can't completely discount, there is certainly an outside chance, but that doesn't seem the most appropriate or likely thing to have happened, on balance.

I have come to the conclusion, after reflecting for a considerable period of time, that it must have been someone else, who broke in through those French windows, through the back, someone maybe from the pub, maybe you knew them? And turned the, the, the gun on you. I just can't let other people think this was you David, it cannot have been you, it wouldn't have been you, ever. It's a matter of honour. It's just so wrong. It would be such a dreadful stain on your character. I must not let that happen to you and I promise you it won't happen. I know what I need to do now, what I must do, in my own mind. I am certain I am doing the right thing, I have thought about it long and hard. Other people may have their doubts and doubt me but that doesn't matter. I am clear about what I need to do.

We will show them, David, we will make sure that you get justice, the justice you deserve and that your name is cleared. It's a matter of principle. I am doing this for you, David. My son.

Chapter 20

May 1981

'Helen, I need to talk to you,' my father says, deliberately.

Oh God, now what? I think. I look at my mother; her eyes are firmly cast down to the floor. No clue. We are all hunched around the fire. I'm back now in Doncaster and spring 1981 never seems to get off the ground, nor move towards summer. The coal fire does not even stretch its warmth to our feet. We are un-comfort-able, the fire knows it.

'Your mother and I have been talking. For quite some time.' I glance over at my mother. No eye contact yet again. A few wordless seconds pass.

'It is a terrible stain on David's character.' He hesitates. His face flushes, a mix of rage and woe battling it out. His eyes bulge slightly. His breaths come a bit gaspily. He is on at least his second gin and tonic. Lunch was a cold collation of meats and sad slaw.

'What do you want me to do?' I really don't understand what he is talking about. Do they want to move? I wait. Give nothing away. Let's see what happens.

'Your mother and I have decided we have no option but to challenge this ... verdict. It is absolutely wrong. It's just like *The Winslow Boy*, remember that? They made a film of it. His parents had to battle the authorities to protect their son and his reputation. It was very hard for them, you know. It will be hard for us, but we've got to stick together.'

I'm struggling to remember – *The Winslow Boy*? A film? Was it maybe a black and white film? 'Remind me of the story,' I ask, playing for time.

He turns his head to the side with a flash of irritation. 'Surely you must remember? The Terence Rattigan play turned into a film. Robert Donat played the role of the leading barrister the family instructs to take on the authorities and prove that their son – what was his name – Dickie? Ronnie? – was falsely accused of stealing a postal order at the academy and expelled. The boy was a teenager. They didn't care about the consequences. It's the same for us. David was older of course, but he's still our son.' He sobs, once. Then he speaks to me, lawyer to lawyer.

'This is more important than anything else. Look, the police were hopeless. They didn't test the gun for fingerprints. Hodgson said that, right in front of the coroner. That Harry Thompson wouldn't even listen to the gunshop owner, who asked him to pick up the shotgun so he could see for himself how impossible it would be for David to do the deed, but he refused. He had six cases on that day, he was in a rush. And what is a "strongest certainty" anyway? Useless. We must appeal against this wholly wrong decision, we've got no option.' He pauses. 'It will affect what people think of David, and it will of course affect the family for the rest of time. It's a stain on his character as well as that of the family. I am determined to address it. David just wouldn't have done this. He couldn't have done it. It is the wrong verdict.'

I am now nearly screaming inside, yelling, *But he must have done! Why can't you see that? Why can't you see?* I can hardly even breathe, I am so afraid that the words will burst out and the whole damned dam-edifice come crashing down.

'We will appeal this,' my father states. 'Until we get the right decision. That if he wasn't murdered, it was an accident.'

'What?' I cry out. This time my response is, shockingly, aloud. Not deliberately, and at least I manage to stop the next word: *Why?*

My mother flinches slightly but says nothing, her gaze on the carpet.

'It's plain to see, isn't it? Let me take you through it,' he continues. 'David was in a good state of mind: your mother and I can attest to that and so can the rector. And that teacher neighbour. The back door was open and there was the cotton bobbin on the back door key I'd never seen before. They didn't even test that for fingerprints as far as I know either. The police never investigated properly whether someone else came into the room. David was drinking, well, we know that and perhaps he had fallen asleep on the couch, and someone, someone else broke into the house and shot him. That's possible. There is no note, no proof that he did it. They can't just assume that, it's wrong in law. The coroner didn't even call on the pathologist as a witness. Helen, we simply have to address this wrongdoing. We will get the right answer.' His eyes are slightly shining now – with tears, certainly, but also with fervour.

I think I mumble 'OK,' though it doesn't matter. This is a matter of principle for my father, for whom doing the right thing is what he does. There is no 'we' involved. I have a strong feeling that I'll end up involved anyway, although I can't yet see how.

●

Later on, Mum is cooking dinner. My father is playing Mendelssohn, 'Fingal's Cave', in the drawing room, and has shut the door to conduct his vinyl orchestra alone. He's on his nth gin and tonic. Mum is cramped over the oven, pulling out a cottage pie while boiling up some peas on the top.

'Can I help?' I ask.

'No, I'm fine.'

If anyone says, 'I'm fine', does it ever actually mean that their health is good, they are happy or at least OK, and that their life is going pretty well, actually? No. It's a code, of course. In my family, 'I'm fine' is code for 'Don't ask, and even if you do you won't get the right answer'. In Spanish, there is a more human and feeling answer: 'Bien, o te digo?', roughly translating as 'Fine. Or shall I tell you?' But we are in Doncaster.

I'm setting the table, and every plate and knife going down seems to clatter loudly, the silence making it noisier. Eventually I ask her, quietly, 'Mum, what do you think about Dad taking this on? Do you think it's a good idea?'

For a while she says nothing. Her energy is low, grief written into her being; the exhaustion of coping with loss. Eventually she says, 'It doesn't really matter what I think, your father is set on it. His view is it was the wrong decision.'

'But don't you think it will rake everything up again, just when we might be starting to, what's his phrase, come to terms with it? Surely, you know … Mum, you can't …' I trail off, seeing the anguish etched into the black pits under her eyes as she looks directly at me.

'Don't ever say that in front of him,' she says, and it sounds almost like an order. 'This is what we are going to do. It's what's happening.'

I make a promise to myself.

'One day…' I search inside. Promises made to yourself are pivotal: they must be kept. If you break a promise to yourself, how can you trust yourself in future? And then how can you possibly learn to trust anyone else?

'One day, David, I will write about it, to say, "This is what happened." If you did take your own life, I don't want that decision taken away from you too.'

I know this is the right thing to do in my gut, although the thought terrifies me. Both my parents would need to be dead, of course, I reassure myself. There is no chance I could ever write about what has happened while they are alive. That will give me time.

•

In the meantime, I still had to answer the question, which came in different forms: how many are there in your family? When I was really messed up, I would flirt with someone until they looked all soft and then tell them. Everything. Cruel, but it felt like it helped because I'd see, reflected in the circles of their eyes, a bit of the hurt that was deep within me. Sometimes I gave an edited account. At the furthest end of the scale, when I didn't want to interact, I might even say, 'I'm an only child.' But I knew that absenting truth could be a lie.

Chapter 21

June 1981

I went back to London to take up the reins of my articled clerkship (nowadays called a training contract) at the City firm of Druces & Attlee. I had been due to start in April of 1981 but, due to my brother's death, I had asked my principal, John Edwardes Jones, if I could have more time off. He gave me an extra month, which became six weeks, but then his attitude toughened and I received a letter saying, 'You must start your work at the firm by the beginning of June, otherwise let us know if you do not wish to take up the position offered and we will look at finding a replacement.'

His words sounded pretty uncaring – and no one who knew him would ever have identified empathy as one of his better-known characteristics – but after the initial shock, I thought his response was fair. I felt that he thought it would be better for me to start work rather than stay at home with two devastated parents. I might well have been wrong in attributing to him a solicitous mindset (although I don't think I was), but his view that I would be better off being away from my parents and starting on my career was spot on, though it took a few months for me to realise.

Starting my new career in one of the loveliest English months was also A Good Thing. The first solicitor I worked with, Christopher Huggins, was as kindly as his surname suggested, and his gentle laugh and thoughtfulness helped a great deal. The wedding of Prince

Charles and Lady Diana Spencer was creating a media frenzy and London was swept up in a mad merry-go-round of believing in the happy ever after.

Moving to London and working now meant that I could not see Nick as much, although our letters and phone calls were regular and loving. He was aiming to persuade his father that the farm could do without him for six months. He came up to see me in London for his twenty-first birthday weekend. I organised hang-gliding lessons for him as a birthday present, so he got his second dream, and we went to see the first UK screening of *Raiders of the Lost Ark* on the big screen in Leicester Square, another mind-blowing experience.

I'd joined another drama group, this time the Actors Institute of New York, which my old school friend Jane, with another friend, Lynne, had brought over the pond to London. A weekend course called 'The Mastery' helped participants to free themselves up in their communication. Nick met some of my new friends in London – think Devonian Gabriel Oak crossed with Crocodile Dundee meets the luvvies. We tended not to spend too long at these gatherings as he attracted attention, male and female.

'Come on Helen, time to go. Let's get out of here.'

The first time Nick came to London I went to Paddington to pick him up, but after that he made his own way to the East End, to my parents' flat in Bow where I was living. 'Helen, I can do this. You're busy. You don't need to run around after me,' he said. 'I'll be all right. I'll make my own way to Bow Road tube, that's where we went last time, wasn't it?'

When he arrived that second time, weathered tan boots striding up the steps, two at a time, to come out through the red-bricked arch onto the busy Bow Road, just by the Bow Church, he looked almost shaken.

Nick threw down his bag, pulled me into his arms and gave me a hug which lasted and lasted. I felt his breathing slowing down, easing, as we, lost humans in an East End bustle, reconnected, country meeting city. He broke away and looked straight into my eyes, as he always did now. There was so much raw honesty between us, almost painfully raw. Eye contact was unfamiliar in my family; perhaps it was just the strangeness. Being next to him felt like being in a direct beam of light; no hiding place.

He grinned then.

'No one talks to anyone or looks at you, Helen. It's the weirdest place, London is.'

'Well if you talk to anyone on the tube, you're the loony, even though it might be them who've lost the plot, not talking. I've had to stop myself from being Northern, you know, like from chatting to people on the underground.'

'There's too many people here, all crowded together, it's no good for them.'

'Maybe you're right, but take care. Don't be friendly. They'll misinterpret,' I replied.

'Well I don't think I've ever seen so many sad-looking people in my life. It must be hell to live here.'

'Kind of hell, but it's sweet, too. I like it. Not for everyone though.' We stepped past a woman selling white heather bundles, doing the London thing of ignoring her.

'Not for me, that's for sure.' He stopped me, again, and put his arms around me. Every time he touched me, especially when we had been apart, I felt that heat.

'Why don't you come to Cornwall, live there, Helen? It's no good for you to live in London, you'll lose your soul. You'll lose your *you*.' He smiled ruefully.

'But tell me, what would I do there? Anyway, I've got to finish off my articles, qualify, get to be a proper solicitor.'

'Proper job,' Nick said, using a West Country saying, which means, broadly, to do something well.

'Anyway you'll be off to Australia soon, my lover,' I retorted, using the Cornish pronunciation, dwelling on the 'errr'. 'So, how's it going, your plans now?'

'My Dad's agreed he could get help on the farm. Can't say he's happy about it. But he might even be able to manage on his own.'

'But he's said yes? He's letting you go?'

'Well, he's not said no. I wanted to tell you when I saw you. I'm getting my freedom. For about six months. I'm planning to head off in September.' He hesitated. 'But what about us, what do you think will happen there, Helen?'

'Let's not think about that. Come on. We've got each other and we're here now.' I kissed him.

We celebrated as we usually did.

I'd read that when an elephant looks as if it's dying, the other elephants in the herd do anything and everything they can to keep the elephant alive, bringing him or her food, spraying them with water, touching and stroking with their trunks, even trying to make love. There was that quality about us: determined that no one else was going to die. We had to make sure each other lived, that's certainly how I felt about it. I knew that for him suicide was enough of an option for him to talk about it, and I wanted to obliterate that option from his world, for him to feel that life was worth living.

I wanted him to open up to the world, travel, meet new people, escape the pressure from his parents – just for a while, as he was certain to go back there. It was in his blood, his lungs, his genes. He needed to go away long enough to find himself, so that when he came back he was choosing the farm from a wholehearted perspective.

Nick knew intuitively how hard it was for me to go on living without my brother. I hadn't talked about suicide – my own – with him or anyone else, but now that my brother had taken his life, for me suicide had become more of a possibility. It was a path now trodden, which David had unwittingly opened up to me as his sister.

Nick and I held on to each other, looked deep into each other's eyes and made love urgently to reaffirm life, our lives, our futures. We clung to each other, hanging on to floating boards after a shipwreck, fighting not to be pulled under.

When the time came for him to leave for Australia, he was to fly from Heathrow. I wanted to take a day off work, but I also didn't want to. I wasn't sure how I could say goodbye and physically let him go, not fall down and plead with him to stay. He didn't need that.

But before that happened, he had another challenge, but one he couldn't tell me about until we saw each other last, in September.

'Dad said to me, "If you leave now, I'm selling the farm. There'll be nothing to come back to." He said it as if he meant it.'

'Oh my God, what did you say?'

'If that's what you want to do, Dad. I'm going anyway.'

'Wonderful, you.'

'Well, it must be worth the risk. But you could come to Australia?' he said.

'I can't. You know I've got no money anyway, just an overdraft. But will you go?' I asked, still unsure.

'It's better if you don't come to the airport. I'll be all right. I'll catch it, I'll be there, dreckly.'

You could translate 'dreckly' as 'directly', but down on the kicking-out leg of Cornwall, it means something like 'in my own time, when I'm good and ready, and don't you tell me what to do, mate'. So more like 'mañana' than 'straightaway'. If Nick had made his mind up, there wasn't much I could do about it.

On the day that his flight was due to leave, I left it as late as I could to go to the office, packing tissues.

'Another cup of tea?' I asked.

'Why don't you get off to your office, Helen. No long goodbyes, we don't need that. Won't be good for either of us. You just go, I'll be off then too. I can pull the door behind me. You don't need to leave me a key,' Nick responded.

'I've got a spare. This is London. You'll need to double-lock it. You can put the keys through the letter box after.'

Why is it that at the most intense times of your life, it's little things that you have to sort out? Our last conversation was about locked doors. But I hadn't got time, there was some dreary meeting which it wouldn't be good for me to miss.

I picked up my briefcase, then dropped it down, pitching into him. Nick still smelled of fresh air and the sea, even having been in London. We had survived. This was the best thing for him, for both of us. His adventures down under would build his confidence, his bravery. He'd be able to do anything after that. It would make him whole.

'Don't say it. Just don't say it. Give me a last kiss, a bleddy good one, and we'll see each other when I get back,' he bade me, before adding, 'If you want.'

I obeyed, but the wrench, the hurt of his leaving, was like a physical tearing.

I walked to the station without turning back. Just focus on each step. But what if he can't cope, if he feels lonely? Is this really the right thing? For him? And what about me? How will I cope?

If I was brutally honest, I also had to admit to myself that there was something of a relief in letting go of being with him; of being so naked, so vulnerable. I would be back to that space, the crater – me – which felt familiar. I would be able to do this. I just had to keep on taking a step forward.

I got to Bow Road tube station, caught the District line and walked to the London Wall office from Mansion House – it was longer, but I could keep on taking steps that way. I got to the office on time for the meeting, took my place, handed out tea and biscuits (I was the only woman and hadn't yet learned not to do that). I couldn't stop looking at my watch.

He must have got to Bow Road now; now he'll be changing on to the Piccadilly line. That'll take about fifty-five minutes, maybe? When he gets to Heathrow, does he know which terminal? But he's left himself hours. Even if he goes wrong, he'll have time to –

'Miss Garlick, are we keeping you from something you deem perhaps more important?'

'Sorry, sir. I'm here. I was a little distracted but yes, of course, I'm with you now.'

'Well don't do it again, looking at your watch. Rather rude. Please tell me you will now give this meeting your undivided attention.'

My body – as in my head – nodded. My mind was silently saying something different, this time specifically and deliberately rude, but I was already being steeped in the art of not showing feelings – better still, not having feelings at all. All of a piece with learning to be a lawyer.

Chapter 22

The main crazy part of my life at that time, another part I couldn't talk much to anyone about, was to do with my father's planned court case to quash my brother's inquest verdict.

When a death is unexplained, the police refer the case to a coroner who decides whether or not to hold an inquest. The purpose of this referral is to enquire into the circumstances surrounding a death and find out answers to some basic questions – who the deceased was, and how, when and where they died – in order to provide the details needed for their death to be registered. It is not a trial. My father, however, thought that it was, in effect: a judgement on David, and on our family about how he died.

I did not want the things I had witnessed at the scene of my brother's death as memories in my head. I wanted to burn the images out of my retinas, my brain. Consciously or unconsciously, I'd blocked out as much as I could. Over the next few weeks, however, I had to see more upsetting images. My father instructed my firm in London to act as agent for the appeal against the original inquest verdict. I'd known I would be caught up in this somehow. Dad told me it was important that this process should be kept in the family; we had to do this as much as possible ourselves, and did I mind if he asked Druces & Attlee to take on the case as London agents?

My dad as a classics scholar used to tell me that there were three different types of questions in Latin. Those that expected a yes (*nonne*), those that expected a no (*num*) and the rest (adding just –*ne* to a word). This was definitely a *nonne* question.

My father's assistant solicitor mostly prepared the case, so my job as the person acting as agent was to deliver the brief to the barrister and turn up to sit behind him at the court hearing. This was before a group of three elderly, white, male Queen's Bench Division (QBD) judges. The barrister Dad had instructed, Brian Lett, who specialised in taking on cases where people were appealing an original suicide inquest verdict, was super bright, kind and pleasant. He told us that on the basis of the evidence put to the coroner the verdict was clearly wrong: the legal test for this had been established in a case he'd acted in previously, which was the reason my father had wanted him to be involved.

The evidence included photographs of the scene of David's death and anything else which could be found to show that the original verdict was wrong. I looked away. Nick Cain was now in Australia – his story was not known to the police, nor, for that matter, would it be to the court.

One thing which had counted in favour of a verdict of suicide first time around was that my brother had taken my dog, Cleo, back to Bill's house in Slade Hooton. David had dropped the dog off without staying to say hello to Bill or stopping to see any of our other old neighbours. He did this about a week before he died. Before the QBD court, the dog food in David's car took on another dimension. It was deemed by the judges to be an important factor that, as David had bought so much dog food, he must have been preparing to live for the next few weeks. Why no police officer ever checked the fridge to see if David had bought food for himself never came up.

Another factor was that no suicide note had been found (true). Nor had any diary entries been found that could tell us anything (not quite true).

I found David's diary at the Salt Box much later, after the court case, when we were sorting out some of his things. Not to throw them away – my parents kept a shrine to my brother in the yellow bedroom for decades, keeping his heavy overcoat, surfboard, fishing rods, Ivanhoe armour and telescope. David had roughly torn out all the diary pages for the six weeks before he died. It was a little lime green diary, probably one of the freebies that my father got for Christmas from accountants and tax advisers and handed out to the family as extra – not always desirable – Christmas presents. There were minimal entries for the first two weeks of 1981. Whom he met and where. What was going on with his motorbikes. Then torn shards, which looked as if the pages had all been torn out together. Then there were only blank pages, for all the days of 1981 that David would not be living.

'Have you seen this?' I asked my father. He looked at it as if it was not unfamiliar and shrugged. 'It doesn't really tell us anything more. Maybe he cut the pages out of his diary as that time was behind him. Some people do that, you know.'

I disagreed inwardly (what about the first two weeks?) and quietly put the diary with my own things.

I learned one thing during this whole process, which later stood me in good stead as a lawyer. Only answer the question that has been put to you. Never anything more. Never volunteer any information that has not been asked for.

If anyone had actually ever asked me, 'Do you know where David's diary is?' or, 'Do you believe your brother took his own life?' or, 'Did you think your brother was depressed?' I would have had to answer yes. But no one ever asked. We were living in a sort of bubble. Other people were embarrassed, or upset, or they just didn't know what to say, so there was more silence around us than talking. Maybe people thought we should be left to grieve. I felt I needed to let Nick go, too. I didn't see how we could have a future together and thought that if I told him when he was in Australia, he'd have the chance to meet someone else. On Bondi Beach, maybe. I wrote him a letter. I was convincing myself I'd be better off alone.

The Christmas after David died was hard. I was trying to live for both David and myself and bought, without even noticing I did, two presents for everyone in my family. I focussed on one step at a time. Don't look up, you might find the next range of hills is too high. Keep your eyes on the ground. Take the next step forward.

The result of the court case on 17 February 1982, and of the excellent advocacy of Brian Lett, was that the original inquest verdict was quashed. A second inquest resulted in an open verdict. My father will say this is still a travesty, but will decide to take no further action. The 'stain' is wiped away.

I decided to see a therapist and was recommended a therapy group by Jane, herself training to be an analytical psychotherapist after giving up being a lawyer. I went to see a man first, but he felt a bit predatory and I wasn't sure I wanted therapy with a man.

Then I went to see Joan, a lovely, elderly, probably Jewish woman, in her therapy rooms near Archway. I was seeing her for about seven months, which I thought should be enough, but the whole psychoanalytic process of leaving therapy becomes jolly hard. You have to have several sessions about why you want to leave and the therapist has to agree. As a client, you are called a patient in psychoanalysis, and that is what you must become. Patience was not one of my virtues and I wanted out. Joan did not want me to finish therapy. She felt I had a lot more that I needed to talk about.

At least she didn't talk to me about 'moving on', one of the stupidest phrases anyone can ever use for someone who is grieving. Where do you move on to, precisely? Taking a step forward is about as good as it gets, maybe even sideways or backwards. If you take a step you get a different perspective. Better than getting obsessed with looking into the crater: it will pull you into its dark void.

We agreed that after her summer holiday I would return to therapy, although the return was still reluctant on my part. Most of our sessions had focussed on my brother; on my blaming my father. She kept asking me, 'Might we perhaps look at your relationship with your mother? Is there anything you would like to explore about your mother, or maybe about your relationships with your women friends?' I looked back at her, horrified. 'Don't bother looking there. It's all about my father and brother.'

In my last session, I confessed my worries of her dying during the summer holidays. She told me – she promised – that she would not die, and said my fears about this were related to my brother dying while I was on holiday in the States. Did I mention that she had emphysema? I found out later that Joan was in training. If she'd had more experience, I doubt she would have made that promise. Rookie error.

She died over the summer. What also came crashing down then was the whole therapeutic edifice of not knowing anything about the therapist's life. I had not paid for my last month's therapy – whether from negligence or upset at Joan's dying, I can't now say. Her husband, her widower, called me to ask me to pay the bill. I did not know she had a husband. He told me how she had died (fighting for breath – they couldn't get her to the hospital quickly enough). He said he had found my number in her papers.

This could well have not been entirely professional, although I was grateful for his explanation. At least I knew what had happened. I was offered more psychotherapy to deal with my therapist's death, but decided I had had quite enough of all that for now. I was twenty-three years old.

I joined a singing group in London and recall performing 'Lean on Me' and leaning deep into what I missed about my brother and how I wanted to help others. I closed my eyes and sang my heart out. When I opened them, I wasn't the only one crying.

I was going to try and live a little, in London. And that's what I did. Let's make that live a lot. It was another thing I'd promised myself.

Chapter 23

David

I don't want anyone to be sad about this. Why should they care? It's just me, my decision. My time's up. I didn't want to live beyond twenty, and guess what? It's just been a question of when. How was the easy bit, once I was at Bothamsall Hall, right? It all fell into place. That owner leaving his filing cabinet open. All I had to do was change the birthdate, and hey presto. So easy. I had to wait until I had the chance, when the gun shop owner was talking to someone else, was distracted, right? I would choose one gun at the shop to claim me. It didn't really matter which. What would the gun care, anyway?

I have friends, from Sheffield, in Cornwall – Geoff, Duncan, Dave, Chris, the Robs, Jimmy, Mike, Simon. But I only talked about it with Nick. He's thought about it too: we're like brothers. I just went cold, Sheffield steel, after I made up my mind. I know I'm going to do it. Nick's dad isn't as hard on him. He's got his future cut out, and he loves those sheep, ha ha, whatever he says.

'Now, sheep, they want to die all the time,' Nick said. 'It's their big ambition in life, dying, see? D-day's got nothing on what sheep can plan out. D for death, for dying. They're always on about it, look into their eyes, see? Lambs, well, they're happy at the start, running around, leaping up in the air with their mates. But once they're grown, sheep not lambs, they get that look, other-worldly like. You look at them. They're planning. Every bleddy morning, they ask themselves the same question: will it be today? That's the one thing they want to do in life, once they're grown. It's not just about the dying, see? They cook up ways to make it as hard as they can, too. Then one day, they wake up, and they think, "That's it. Today's D-day. Thank bleddy God. Goodbye bleddy dog." They've worked out the best place, the awkwardest place to die, toughest of all for the farmer, as if his life isn't bleddy hard already. Farthest corner of the field, in the stream, two legs caught up under an old gate, right tucked under the bloody thorns, in the nettles, hard as can be to get their dead, fat, wet, stinking, swollen, maggoty body out, loaded on the tractor and away. You can't even bury them on the farm, these days.'

Don't think about Nick. I need a clear head. I am tired. They say that when you want to go to sleep you think about sheep and I'm thinking about them right now. Ha. I'm no lamb anymore, maybe I'm a bloody sheep and I'm going to go to sleep for a long time, for ever, but I won't make it that hard to find me. Helen won't find me, she's in the bloody States anyway, what does she care? That next-door neighbour? I haven't seen him. Maybe Dad. Not Mum. She won't be the one. I can't think about that. I might … Not Grannie either. Anyway, she can't get out so much. Grandpa's dead. Wonder if I'll see him after…? It'll be Dad. When they're back from holiday. I've got to do it before they get back. Time's ticking.

Maybe no one … will find me for a while, my body will rot, the flies will land and shoot in their eggs, the maggots might get at me, too. They'll get bloody drunk and have a bloody hangover from hell if I knock back enough; enough so I won't feel any more. That's a laugh. Do maggots get hangovers? It won't hurt.

Cleo needed sorting. I had to get rid of her. She kept looking at me, wouldn't leave my side. She knew. I couldn't look her in the eye. I should have dropped her off at Bill's, but I couldn't look at him either. He'd have known. He might have tried to stop it. Cleo will be OK with Bill, he'll look after her. And they won't read anything in the diary, no one will, that's gone now, or the last six weeks, anyway. Linda? Never. Cold, that one. And Stella? She said she loves me, but it would never work out. It never does for me.

Some people could spot it in my eyes, in my face. Some people must have seen it, is that why some of them stopped talking to me? That teacher said I had a suicide wish in my report, and it was only because I hadn't done my homework and failed some exams. He saw it. I was the living dead. Years before, that was.

I'm not responsible for anyone else, never mind myself. Better off dead. It'll be easier for all of them, they'll get on with their lives, forget me. I'm not good enough. They stopped talking to me: no one has anything left to say. I didn't know how to break it. If anyone said

David, aged 20

anything to me, they got at me. I got no peace. So I'm going to make my D-day plan, like the sheep. Ha bloody ha.

It's better, knowing it's happening now. It didn't even need that much planning. It's the easiest thing to do. Almost too easy. That'll teach him for leaving that filing cabinet open. It's not my fault. Maybe I wouldn't have even done it if the certificate wasn't there. But it was. And that changed it all. It's set now. I'll be dead, see? No coming back from that. I'm going to do it right, not like the lads who shot Dusty. She must have been in agony. No. Clean and quick. No shaking, no faltering. Hold true.

I'm drunk, I couldn't be doing this stone cold sober. That would be really mad. I need to be really good, proper drunk. I planned for that. I got the gun out and left it on the sofa while I got more beers in my belly. I walked round it a few times, the gun, picked it up now and then, put it down again. Not yet. Not now. Soon, though. Soon enough. I had some more to drink, but the beer wasn't hitting the spot at first, not hard enough. I got some wine, might as well open them all, saves time. Though whose time am I saving? Don't think about it.

It went down easy. Sliding down, quicker hitting the spot. Feeling warm in my gut. I'll have as much as I bloody well want, no next-day hangover this time. Need to aim straight though, so no passing out. Keep my head is what I need to do. Ha ha, that's a bloody laugh.

Life stinks, might as well be dead. Try it out. See how that works out. Can't be worse than this life, can it?

And then. In a second or less. Bang. Just as I'm doing it, I'm thinking, I might not do this, or I might. Think of Dusty. Don't hesitate on pulling the trigger. Enough thinking. It's time.

Part Two
Three
Endings

O time, thou must untangle this, not I.
It is too hard a knot for me t'untie.
  William Shakespeare *Twelfth Night*

When the present begins to fracture,
there is room for the future to be written.
  Jessica Andrews *Saltwater*

Chapter 24

Autumn 1983, the Salt Box

My parents were still going through the motions at this stage of life, two and three quarter years since my brother died. Get up, brush your teeth, eat breakfast, read a paper, work, drink, have lunch, drink, work, drink again, have dinner, go to bed. The drinking did not start before 12 p.m., that was a rule.

I knew Nick Cain might be in the pub that night. Casually, I'd asked Julie, Mum's housekeeper, if he was around. 'Oh, yes, he's come home from Australia,' Julie confirmed. 'Months ago, I think. He's back with Caitlin now you know, since he came home. Still wild, though. No change there,' she volunteered. 'I sometimes see him going to the pub.' Julie's house was three doors away from the Bullers Arms, although she rarely visited the pub. She and her family were Methodists.

I wanted to talk more to Julie about Nick, but I could not. I couldn't speak of my relationship in front of her anyway, nor in front of my partner James, who had come through the door.

I talked of everything except the person, the man, who was on my mind all day that day. It was the end of October, a time when heaven and earth close in on each other, the layers between this life and the next thinning.

'How about before dinner we all go down to the pub? To the Bullers? It will get us all out a bit and it will be nice.' I ventured.

'Dinner's ready, no time to go now,' said my mother. 'And anyway we've got plenty in here. Enough to sink a battleship.' I revived my plea after dinner. My father fell for it. 'Well you, James and I can all go down? Perhaps not your mother, if she doesn't want to?'

We looked over at my mother, his wife. She shook her head. 'I don't. I'll stay and clear up.'

'Oh no, Monica, we'll take care of that,' responded James, smoothly.

'All right then. I'll have a nice sit down.' A nice sit down was my mother's ambition most days. She sat down with her pain and her grief and did a crossword, or worked through her current book of quizzes and puzzles, soothing herself her way. She became pretty darned good at it too.

The three of us headed towards the pub. I did not see Nick at first but I sensed, animal-like, that he was there. I could smell him. I was on high alert. I knew that he was walking towards me while I had my back to him, but he sheered away as he approached. I felt that too.

'Wasn't that Nick Cain?' said my father, who had a better view of the pub.

'Was it?' I didn't exactly lie.

James bought the first round, and we said hardly anything to each other, except that James would almost certainly have talked about something to smooth things over. I kept on seeing Nick out of the corner of my eye, with other friends of David's, including Mike, who approached us.

'Helen. It is you? Well of course it is. I just didn't know you were coming down this way. How are you? Come over and have a drink? What about your Dad? What about Geoffrey? And – your friend?' This was Mike talking. 'What about him?'

Nick Cain had joined Mike now.

'Yes, what about him, your friend?' echoed Nick, his lip curling. After a few seconds, he laughed. The others did then, too.

'Oh we're all right, thanks, we've just had a round,' I said. 'How are you?' looking at Mike, wanting to ask Nick.

'Mother's been OK, had a bit of a cold but she's getting over it. Can't complain you know,' said Mike, chatty as usual.

Nick dragged on his cigarette, tilted his head back and parted his lips, blowing out the smoke harshly, a funnelled smoke-shaft snaking towards the ceiling.

He paused, before turning slightly towards me.

'What are you like, Helen, coming here?'

No one else said anything. I said nothing, frozen. He spun his body away to walk back to his table.

I went back to my family group and tried to chat. It was half an hour before I was anywhere near him again. The physical distance closed when I went to go to the loo. I felt his eyes on me as I left the room, turning towards the pub cloakroom, off a white-painted corri-dor with a slate flagstone floor, pictures of hunting scenes on the walls. To the right were the toilets, to the left was the front way out of the pub.

When I left the loo, I could see smoke being blown up to the night sky from someone outside the doorway. My choice was to turn back into the pub's warmth, to my father and a man who loved me, and to other friends. Or go outside, step across the

The author in 1983

slate flags, to a man who still held my heart at the end of a rope, hooks implanted. The line pulled tight, the hooks bit in deeper.

I stepped through the doorway and turned towards him. Without others to observe me, I could look at him directly. Nick was just as beautiful as I remembered. But now there was no gentleness. I felt grazed by his eyes.

'Do you want to go for a drive, Helen? We could talk, away from this lot. If you want. My Land Rover's at the back. I'll wait. You can go and see,' he paused. 'Them. If you like.'

I walked back like an automaton to my father and James. 'I'm going to be a while. You go back home. I'll see you there later. I need to talk to someone. Yes, it's him. Don't worry. And, well, sorry about this.'

James's eyes searched out mine but I would not look at him. 'I won't be long.'

'Helen?' he appealed. I was gone already.

As quickly as I dared, I ran back towards the back of the pub, the car park near Under Lane. He was there, the engine turning over, diesel reverberation throbbing into life. I got in beside him, sweeping away twine, tools and screwed up invoices, cloths, sheep medicine, an old blanket, work boots. It smelled of wet dog and mud. Without looking at me, he put the Defender into gear before I'd closed the door. The vehicle shot sturdily forwards, then sharply to the left on to the road. I lurched to the left, pushed my weight back to the right, banging the door shut.

●

'Where do you want to go?' I ask.

'You'll see,' he says. I don't believe he knows. He is driving blindly, looking at the road but almost unseeing, eyes glassy. He knows this land, these lanes, this country, like he knows his own hands.

We drive for several minutes in silence. He breaks it first.

'Do you want music? I can see if we can get Radio 1 on. Or maybe you're into Radio 2 by now. You're that much older than me, if I remember that bit right.'

I'm stung. 'Radio 1 is fine. I'm not that old.'

'Really? That man you're with in the pub. What's his name?'

'James.'

'He looks like he'd get on with your Dad. Like they're not that far apart. Lawyers both of them, aren't they? Bleddy lawyers.'

James is seven years older than me. Twenty years younger than my dad. I don't take the bait. I breathe out and say nothing for a while.

'How are you these days? How's it going?' I break the silence.

'How do you think it's fucking going? You bloody well chucked me when I was stranded in Australia. Thousands of miles away. I was on a bloody sheep farm in the middle of the outback. What do you think that felt like?'

'I don't know,' I say, miserably. 'Bad, I expect. I'm sorry.'

'Christ. You say sorry, Helen. Sorry. As if that fixes anything,' he snaps.

'I said sorry before. In the letter. I meant it. I'm sorry I hurt you.'

'All your fucking promises. Turned out to mean nothing.'

The noise of the Landie engine fills the cab.

'Are you back with Caitlin?' I shout. Inept to ask but worse to say nothing. I can't find anything right to say.

'Yes,' he roars back. 'She had me back. She's a good girl. I've had others. Tourists, in the summer. They're easy. But it's Caitlin, she's my girl.' He looks at me. 'She's always been the girl for me. It was never you.'

He carries on driving through twisting country roads with high stone-walled hedges, drives up a lane and parks by a tree bereft of leaves, ivy tangling and strangling the tree in a long, slow struggle. He yanks on the handbrake. It is suddenly, deafeningly, quiet. Not even an owl. I look out at the stars, glass shards, cold and dead, gadzillions of miles away. He leans in and kisses me, roughly. I respond, more out of guilt. I suddenly, desperately want to be back at home. Everything feels wrong.

This is so far from what I'd imagined, though why would it be anything else? I curse myself; all of this is my fault. I saved him, though he saved me too. It was a joint rescue effort. And then I said goodbye. Did I imagine some kind of reconciliation, a happy ending, or that at least we could be friends? We are further apart than strangers. We say little. There is no more healing to be done, only the potential for more wounds. After a while he starts up the engine again and drops me back at the Salt Box.

·

I did not hear his voice again for thirty-six years.

When I think of my brother I often think of Nick Cain. Our relationship sprang up in the ashes of my brother's death, amidst the phantom of Nick's future death – mine too, if we hadn't been able to grip onto life. It wouldn't have worked out long term. We were too different. That's my left brain speaking and this time, for once, it is quite right.

Endings aren't always pretty, even in stories. Anyway, it's never just about the man, the loved one, the other, is it?

Chapter 25

July 2014

My dad's decline into dementia was a pitiful thing, and tricky for those around him to handle. He said his memory was absolutely fine, and he had ways of covering up the fact that facts were slipping away from him, more recent facts especially. Dad forgot people's names, so he took to calling people 'My old friend'. He would ask people things like 'How are your ... children ... where they are now?' This also included my children, his beloved three grandchildren, on occasions. My mother knew and talked to me about his decline, in whispers usually, but my father had lost none of his bombastic nature, so challenging him or getting him to talk to a doctor about what was going on seemed impossible, as usual.

Dad was drinking heavily. Cheap wine, whatever was on special offer at Sainsbury's. Every evening. More if it was a special occasion – when other people were around, or a meal out. His constitution was extraordinary. I have seen him down several gin and tonics (mostly gin), two bottles of wine and half a bottle of whisky, then be up early the next morning, knock back a full English breakfast and carry on. His doctor, who died a good few years before my father, said, 'I can't believe the results. I had to check them in case there was some mistake. You are a lucky man, Geoffrey. Your heart is fine. Your cholesterol is fine. Your blood pressure is up so you need hypertension tablets. Other livers would have packed up by now.

Frankly, Geoff, it's not fair.' My father smiled, perhaps thinking he had beaten the odds.

The pickling of both of my parents started relatively late in life. Neither of them drank much alcohol, if any, when they were younger – my mother always preferred water – but in the 1970s alcohol (there were fewer addictive drug choices then widely available) was attractively racy; smart. Drinking had associations for my parents with the romance of Europe and beyond. The two questions that I would (sadly) most often associate with my father were 'Would you like a drink?' and 'What would you like to drink?' I cannot remember him asking me 'How do you feel?' even though I knew he loved me. Every time we said goodbye, he always said, 'We're thinking of you.'

But I was worrying more about him, their drinking, especially his, and my mother. Once, I braved it.

'Dad, I'm really worried about how much you're drinking and the effects on your health. You seem to be having more nowadays. Is there a way we could talk about this?' I asked, while the adults were all still at the lunch table in the Salt Box. He pushed back his wooden captain's chair, scraping it hard against the Cornish grey slate floor, stood up, stared me in the face for a few seconds of heart-stopping silence and snapped, 'How dare you!' He then banged out into the garden, carrying his chair and his beloved newspaper, muttering loud enough that we could all hear how badly children treat their parents these days and how there was just no respect left any more.

We watched him stomp over the lawn to a place beneath the cooking-apple tree, laden down with fruit, in the furthest part of the garden from the house. He placed the chair with its back, and his, towards us and sat down, opening up *The Sunday Telegraph* to dive in, the only visible sign of his continuing rage being the furious way he was running his hair through his fingers, pulling the long strands over his bald patch, Arthur Scargill-style.

'Leave him,' my mother said. 'You need to get ready to go back home. And go and get the children ready.' My husband and I escaped upstairs to get the bags and the children. When the car was full of all the stuff we were taking back, we looked at each other and went back to the kitchen and the garden, the children following on behind.

My father had not moved. 'Let's just call out goodbye to Grandpa, shall we?' I said, maybe too brightly. 'He's very involved with his newspaper.'

'Goodbye, Grandpa, Byeee!' chimed little voices towards an unmoving back. 'Bye Dad,' I called. 'See you soon,' hoping I wouldn't, but knowing I would anyway.

'It's no use, Helen, he'll never change,' said my mum.

But change is constant, and if a crisis isn't managed it will erupt in another way. For him it was falling over a kerb when going to get his daily paper. Dad broke his hip, was hospitalised, went cold turkey, returned to the flat after my mother had cleared out all the bottles, but still deteriorated. Inexorably, he had to go into care, to a home which specialised in dementia, my father having a form most likely caused by his alcohol abuse. You don't fool the body in the end.

I had learned over the years of being a family lawyer and mediator, and being interested (as well I might be) in trauma and family relationships, that to understand anyone you need to hop up to the next generation and see what was going on there. My father's parents were ill-suited and it was an unhappy marriage by most accounts. My father had been brought up with the belief that it was the appearance of things that counted most, and he struggled to put on the show which must have cost him dearly underneath.

Financially, too. In a rare moment of openness, he told me that back in the seventies, when South Yorkshire was devastated by the miners' strikes and the bosses' struggle for control, backed by Ted

Heath, my father refused to let any one of his staff go and kept them in full employment. He built up an overdraft of £25,000 which led to the bank forcing him to sell Slade Hooton Hall at auction for £75,000 back in the late seventies (they couldn't initially sell the piano but it was eventually bought to be made into a cocktail cabinet). Twenty years later, the Hall reputedly sold for more than a million. Bank managers are often fools, my father said, adding them to his list of dislikes.

By the summer of 2014 he was reduced to a fraction of himself, kept in a care home for demented souls which he probably detested, although he never said so. He said little. Occasionally he would spout a bit of Latin, the last few drops from the fount of a clever mind, but he was mostly interested in eating jelly babies and liquorice allsorts, after he had to give up alcohol. His body was curling in on itself, the bones of his feet becoming more like claws. He had not walked for several months by 8 July 2014, when a late-night call came in from my father's care home, after I had been to see a Pink Floyd tribute band in Oxford.

'Your father has been taken into Stoke Mandeville Hospital. He hasn't been passing urine properly. He hasn't been eating much either. He's gone to hospital as a precaution, but don't worry.'

I phoned my mother to tell her. 'Let's go to the hospital early in the morning, Mum. They say it's not too serious. The hospital visit is just to check things out. See if you can get a good night's sleep. I'll pick you up very first thing tomorrow.'

After collecting my mother at 6 a.m. on the way into hospital, we went to accident and emergency and were shown to a cubicle. My father was in a far worse state than I was prepared for. He looked frightened. He was lying on a bed, with tubes attached, breathing through an oxygen mask, fighting for his breath, his eyes latching on to mine, his breathing coming noisy, deep and quick, but not seeming to reach him inside.

'It's all right Dad,' I reassured him. 'It'll be all right.' But it really wasn't. The A and E doctors informed us he had kidney failure, pneumonia and sepsis on top of his dementia. He wasn't speaking at all by now. He hadn't been walking for months.

We got the news, then went back to see him. I smiled at him reassuringly. He seemed to recognise me and the panic in trying to catch his breaths maybe eased.

On the night shift, the registrar in charge was a sensible, kind woman, Dr Campbell. She came to tell us that in her view, after all the tests they had run, my father had not long to live. There would not be enough time to get him to a hospice. She would see if she could find us a bed on a ward which would be quiet, ideally his own room. Did we have any questions?

'He needs pain relief, what can you give him. Please? I don't want him to be scared like this.' Pain relief – morphine – materialised. My father seemed to relax more. We stayed by his side, waiting for a bed to become free.

At the staff changeover time at 8 a.m., another dilemma presented itself in the shape of an older male A and E consultant who came bursting into the room ordering staff to get my father ready for theatre. What was going on? My mother and I exchanged an anxious glance. I knew she wouldn't say anything. I needed to say what were both thinking and argue a case for compassion, not intervention. This will not be what they want to hear. They are primed to save lives, be a hero, keep people on the planet as long as they can.

'Hold on please, can we just pause a moment. I've been told that my father hasn't long to live. Why do you want to do this?'

The consultant's response was, 'I need to make him comfortable. The blockage from his kidneys could be relieved with a relatively minor operation. It would need a general anaesthetic, though. I need you or your mother to sign some papers for him to give your consent.'

'And quite apart from his dementia, and never mind his kidney failure, what about his pneumonia, and sepsis?'

'We can manage that in theatre.'

'So assuming that he actually survives the surgery, how long would that give him?'

'Well, I would estimate a minimum of two weeks, at the very least. Possibly quite a bit more than that.'

'So, can I get this right?' I snapped. 'You are planning to take a scared, demented man, my father, into surgery to give him maybe another two weeks of life when he has no quality of life anyway? He does not speak or communicate. He barely eats. He doesn't walk. I have not seen him smile in years. He doesn't know what's going on. He is in pain. It must be really hard living in his body. I refuse to agree. My mother agrees with me.'

We both looked over at my mum, who nodded decisively, and said, 'I fully agree with my daughter.'

'Look. He's getting near the end, isn't he?' I persevered. 'That's what we've been told by your colleague. He's eighty-three. We don't want him to have to go through an operation. It will scare him even more. It's not right. What he needs right now is peace and quiet. A chance to die with some dignity. No heroics here, please.'

And then I adopted a phrase of my father's that I've heard him say hundreds of times. It can come in handy, especially with doctors.

'And I am a solicitor.'

The glimmer of excitement I thought I spotted in the consultant's eyes at the prospect of surgery to save this unsavable man faded. He must have known there was no point in this operation. My father could well die on the operating table. That would not look good on his statistics. There was no need to point this out though; some things are better left unsaid. He went over to confer with his colleagues. Perhaps he didn't want to lose face. One of the more junior doctors came back about ten minutes later.

'We've decided that in all the circumstances, and given the family's express wishes, we will not operate at this time.'

The words smacked of lawyerliness. Maybe my being a lawyer had shunted them into having to get some legal advice? No matter; it was a relief. The important thing was that my father wouldn't be hacked around and spend his last few hours or days dealing with the after-effects of an operation. Doctors do not always seem to be wise in the art of dying: their priority is to keep the living alive as long as possible. When someone dies, they tend to see this as a failure, despite the ultimate inevitability of death.

Now this medical battle was over and things started to settle, I called my children to tell them the news. Death, or the prospect of death, was sadly familiar to them, but they had not been able to visit him much in the care home. Too upsetting: he did not recognise them. I wondered if that would make their grief and loss more complex.

My children came over to see their grandfather and hold his hand. They said loving words, 'Thank you for being a wonderful Grandpa.' 'We love you.' 'Goodbye.' They told a few stories about times they remember him as a grandfather. They cried, of course they cried. However distant he had become from them, from us all, in the last few years, he was the only grandfather they had known. Then they had to leave; their lives called them. They walked out of A and E, arms tight around one another. I had a pang, feeling the absence of a brother's arm around me, of us comforting each other at our father's death. I sighed. No point in mourning that long-gone loss.

A helpful nurse tracked down a bed in a ward for my father, the porter came to collect him for his last journey, and we headed off to a cool, relatively peaceful ward, painted linen white. It was warm outside and the window was open, to let in the sounds of happy summer life. A breeze gently blew into the room, stirring up the curtains like sails. Especially in the setting of a big, busy town hospital, this was almost a healing space. We were especially lucky to have an earth-angel going by the name of Michael, who was assigned to look after my father, along with the rest of the patients on his ward. He pulled the curtains around Dad's bed to give us some privacy.

Michael got us each a cup of tea and brought a sponge for my father's forehead and a little lollipop sponge with a cup for occasional sips of water. Michael observed my father's breathing and his blood pressure: now on a downward curve, as was his heart rate. His mortal decline was beepingly measured on the monitor to which my father was attached. We kept looking at the electronic monitor instead of being able to focus on the human, my father. The beeping added to the anxiety. 'Do we still need to have this?' I queried. 'Please?' Michael acknowledged its pointlessness and quietly went off to see one of the doctors, to get the all-clear to remove the monitor.

Michael then told us with immeasurable kindness and warmth that he would leave us in peace but if we needed anything, to please call him. He would just come back to ensure that my father had enough pain relief.

We didn't know how long my father had. Could be a day or more, could be a few hours. Or less. Like birth, death comes in its own time. My mother and I took up our posts at opposite sides of the bed, a shared vigil for my dying father; her dying husband. Our task was to say our goodbyes and let him go, while he let go of this world.

My father was on high doses of morphine. His eyes sometimes rolled in their sockets in his opiate-induced state, but he was calmer, more relaxed. Accepting. He said nothing, but there was a quality of peace in the room which was palpable. It felt sacred. It was gentle, not the bruling, loaded silences of the past.

I held and stroked my father's hand and told him I loved him and I was grateful for his being my father. I was. Without him, I would not have been born. I'd brought a book of John Betjeman poems, his favourite, and read a couple to him. I think I detected a glimmer of a smile. My mother asked me if I wanted to go off and get a tea and a break. I did. I asked her if there was anything she wanted to say to him. She shook her head and looked at the carpet. She was polite when Michael came in, but spoke little. We went out together for a few minutes, returning quickly.

My father's breathing was slowing. He took fewer breaths and most were detectably fainter, then every so often he grasped for a deeper breath, hanging on to life, before lapsing back into soft, shallow breaths. I watched him closely, trying to decipher whether he wanted me to be there or not. When I went away briefly, his face moved a little towards the curtain where I'd left, and it was twisted in the same position when I got back. I sat next to him again and he settled more, his head moved back to the centre of his pillow. I held his hand.

After maybe another half an hour, his breaths were slower, fainter; longer spaces between them. Knowing, though I don't know how, I said to my mother, still silent, 'I think it won't be long now. Is there anything else you want to say to him, Mum?'

She shook her head, moved over towards him and kissed him, three short, quick bursts of kisses on his forehead and she whispered goodbye. I kissed his forehead too. It was cold, a little clammy, getting paler. Mentally I surrounded my father with white light.

'Be safe, go towards the light, be peaceful, go in peace, see the light, move towards it,' I told him, softly. 'You will be with David soon.' I focussed my being on letting him go and bringing as much light into the room to surround him as I could. We waited.

One breath. Then what seemed like a few minutes, perhaps only one, when he didn't breathe. I caught my own breath. Had he gone? My father suddenly gathered some energy into himself, took a bigger breath and then – jumped. Not physically. But just as you would gather up all your energy when you want to jump high off the ground, he jumped. There's no other way I could describe it. He jumped out of this world and into the next. No more breaths. We waited. Still no more. His complexion began to go waxy.

'I think he's gone,' I said to my mother. She raised her eyes from the carpet where they had been burrowing for most of the morning and gave a tiny sob.

'At last,' is what I thought she said.

It had been an amazing privilege, a gift, to be at my father's side for his death. It was one of the most extraordinary events in my life.

I spent a few more moments mentally speeding his soul towards the light, towards peace. Then I went to find earth-angel Michael.

Michael checked his pulse, his breath: nothing. Michael said, 'Yes, he's gone,' and went to find a doctor. She certified his death. Our vigil had lasted a little over four hours.

My father's ashes were buried in my brother's grave a few months later. Mum rigidly insisted that he be cremated rather than buried, despite his express preference. I felt I could not force a choice of the dead on the still living, my surviving parent. I still feel bad about that.

Chapter 26

November 2017, Mill Court, Waddesdon

'Do you mean it, Mum?' I say, as calmly as I can.

'What does Judy think?' she asks.

'Judy thinks it's the right thing to do, Mum,' I say, paraphrasing Judy's clear guidance to me on boundaries ('You've got far too much on. She's sacked those carers you organised for her, every time, and she can't keep on saying "Well, I've got Helen." If she can't cope, she'll have to go into a home.').

Judy, my mother's sister, seven years her junior, still lives life in fifth gear, though she's nearly 80. She was a second-hand car dealer, learned to fly a plane and paraglide, has a brimmingly fruitful garden and walks every day. She and her husband Tony are besotted with one another after decades of being together. She wears her heart on her sleeve. Very different from my mother.

'And Gwen?' Gwen is my mother's oldest friend, in the sense of the longest-lived friendship still alive. She has been a great support to me with my parents these latter years.

'Gwen too,' I respond.

'I'll miss the Wednesday Club.'

The Wednesday Club is a day care centre run in Waddesdon by the sainted Paula and helpers, to which my mum initially refused to go and then, once she had gone, became obsessed by and talked of little else.

'I know, but there could be activities every day at your new care home, not just Wednesdays.'

She sighs. 'OK.' The OK is stronger now, but at least it's still an OK. The giving up of the independences that make life tolerable for her is not easy. But she is worrying us. Like the time when she phoned up (her mobile phone was charged for once) a few months ago.

'Helen, I'm just giving you a call. I'm in a lay-by, in the car. I've forgotten where the brake is. I thought it best to pull over.' Small mercy. I give her a quick description. 'Oh, of course. I'll be fine now.' But would other road users? Eventually the memory clinic tells her she'll need to take another test to carry on driving, and she decrees she is not happy driving anymore and gives her car to my younger daughter.

The most poignant memory loss was when I took her, along with the rest of the family and my fiancé Tim, to North Cornwall, to visit the Eden project and to see my brother's grave, where her husband's ashes are now buried. She glanced over at me and Tim by David's grave while her grandson Will supported her to walk around the graveyard, she holding on to his arm, my daughters alongside.

'What are they looking at?' she queried.

If anyone ever asks, my mother tells people that she has Alzheimer's. That is not quite true. Her actual diagnosis is mild cognitive disorder, but the medical letter in which this is set out unhelpfully has the word 'Alzheimer's' in its heading. My mother does not wish to read the remainder of the letter, or even listen when I read out to her that she has instead the milder version of memory impairment. She says she has Alzheimer's.

'Now Mum, I am going to suggest that I look around Sussex, where Tim and I will be moving to soon, as that will work better longer term. Do you agree?'

'That sounds sensible. Will you tell the home I have Alzheimer's?' she asks.

I call Judy on the way back. 'You've got no option, sweetheart. It's time.'

I had emailed Gwen last night. Gwen still lives in Sheffield with her wife Maud: both have been in poor health for the last year or two. I come back to read her response on my laptop.

Hello Helen,

I agree with you entirely. Pip has emailed me every day for the last week, and before that it was at least 3 times a week.

I've tried to support her but there's a limit to what I can do too. I can sympathise with her but I don't think she's safe on her own anymore.

Good luck when you talk to her. She can be very manipulative and even stubborn. At times. I think you know this though.

Love Gwen x

I go and visit a prospective care home. Mum would be in her own room, with her own bathroom, overlooking a garden which faces out towards the sea, with her own balcony and plenty of activities. The staff are warm and homely; there's home-cooked food. Many of the inmates have dementia.

I call Aunty Judy again. 'Look Helen, you focus on you and your family now. You had breast cancer last year, what was it? A nine-hour op? My sister can't just keep on saying "I've got Helen". You and your family: that's your priority. As long as she's safe and warm. She won't be happy, you know that. But she'll probably settle to it.'

Tim and I arrange to pick my mother up to take her to the home.

She stands waiting by the front door, her coat and hat on, her stick by her side. I hold her hands – barely warm – and search her face. Her eyes were once cornflowers, called bachelor's button, and the sclera bright white. The cornflowers look grey now, and her eyes are cobwebbed with red. But not fully red, which is what happens when she has a psychotic episode, so that's something. Underneath her eyes the bags are etched darkly. Her freckled skin is wafer-thin, crinkly, with marks where cancerous skin patches once were. Mum's Nordic cheekbones still jut defiantly, and her straight Roman nose and curved Cupid's bow lips give archaeological clues that this was a beautiful face. Her hair is cut short now, always.

'I haven't slept,' she says. 'But I'm ready.'

The estate car's boot is soon filled up with what she wants to – and can – bring with her, from her diminished life. She hands me a canvas bag. I peek inside. All our wrapped-up Christmas presents and cards are carefully packed, with bottles of red wine and port which she will never touch as she gave up drinking in 2007, and a list of who gets which present.

I tear up.

'Mum, that's so sweet of you. Thank you! You'll be out for Christmas anyway – we've rented the house in St Leonards to go to for the whole family. All five children! And Tim's brother. It will be lovely. It's only two weeks till we'll collect you for Christmas.'

Mum locks the door to her flat and hands me the key, together with a white plastic carrier bag, with stuff inside. 'Keep that. It's for you. No use to me anymore,' she says.

We walk, with her stick, to the car. She hangs on to my arm tightly, but otherwise shows no emotion, and says nothing.

Mum is getting into the front seat, while Tim is about to go in the back, me driving. He and I are standing to help her into the car. I pull the front seat strap over and click it in.

'Just a minute,' she says. 'Hold on. I've forgotten something. I need to go back. I want to get my white dress to wear it to your wedding.'

Tim and I exchange a glance. My look pleads. This is the same white dress which made an unwelcome appearance at my first wedding in 1989. Nearly thirty years on, her dress is infected with mould, never mind who wears white at a wedding? Tim reassuringly puts his hand, a steady, warm hand, on the base of my spine and gently strokes my back. His gesture calms me more than anything else. I have long waited for the touch of this hand.

'Now, Monica,' Tim begins, turning towards my mother with a smile, his gentle but firm BBC voice quelling any argument. 'Helen and I would love to buy you a beautiful new coloured dress, perfect for the wedding.'

'All right then,' my mother responds, with one of her rare and wonderful smiles. 'Let's go.'

We take my mother to the care home and settle her in, put her things where she wants them. Including a pile of papers, which she calls 'my memoir' and which she's placed on her bed. Right on top of the paper pile is a white, already used and opened envelope, with her handwriting on it, like notes.

While she's in the loo, I idly look at the envelope. Her writing takes a while to work out – her M looks more like a Greek pi, her capital I looks like a J and her lower-case l is looped – but I can make out the first sentence.

'I am and will always not be the same but be different.'

The bathroom door suddenly opens and Mum shuffles out. I put the envelope down, before she sees me, I think, and I carry on sorting things out.

'What's in the plastic bag you gave me, Mum?' I ask, instead.

'It's my jewellery. I didn't want to leave it in the flat, nor here either. You have it.'

•

Eight days after admission, my mother unexpectedly dies, on the shortest day of the year. The day before, Tim and I visited her for a roast lamb lunch (her favourite) and she said, 'Thank you very much for everything you have done.'

The manageress calls me in the morning. 'I am so sorry, we just can't believe it here. She was such a lovely lady. We went in to check on her at 6 a.m., she was sleeping peacefully, then by the next routine check at 7 a.m. she had died. We called the ambulance and they tried resuscitating her but she had already gone.'

As Mum died so soon after being admitted to the care home, without having been recently visited by a doctor, I must identify her at the undertakers where her body has first been taken, and a coroner must again be involved before her death certificate is issued. It seems excessive. My mother was elderly, with underlying health problems (hypertension, skin cancer, dementia, panic attacks and, as it turns out, congestive heart failure) and had been waiting to join her much loved son for nearly thirty-seven years.

It seems sad that her lifeless body must now be cut open to prove why she died, but I have no say. It is the law, a legal procedure, a form of protection against deceivers and murderers.

I go to collect the rest of her things, as requested. The care home staff are tender-hearted and don't rush me, but her room is needed. The sea-facing room with a balcony will soon have a new occupant. There is a waiting list.

Part Three
New
Beginnings

*The past is beautiful because one never realises
an emotion at the time. It expands later,
and thus we don't have complete emotions
about the present, only about the past.*
Virginia Woolf, *Diaries Vol. 3*

*Love is not the least bit illogical or random,
but actually an ordered and wise recipe for
survival. The need for connection is our
first and most primary human instinct.*
Dr Sue Johnson, *Love Sense*

Chapter 27

A tiny girl who never took a breath.

One single shot, shrouded in darkness.

One leap, from a demented world into the next.

One broken heart giving out, switching off the light.

We four, or five, depending on how you count a life, are now down to one.

●

This one, on 17th February 2016, the same day of the year as the court case in 1982, woke up about an hour ago in the recovery room of the new, blue, Royal London hospital after an eight and a half hour operation to remove my left breast and reconstruct another in its place. My breast cancer surgeon is called Mr Anthony Peel, my plastic surgeon Miss Caroline Payne, a classic bit of nominative determinism.

Fifty centimetres of sewn-up skin trace the arc of a thin-lipped Joker's smile from my left hip to my right. I was tempted to skip my routine mammogram on 4th January 2016, so soon after the seasonal break and with work piling up in the office, but something made me show up. If I hadn't, I might not have lasted long on the planet at all. The mammogram and other tests revealed two masses of stage 2 cancer deep inside, near the bone. My brother-in-law David (from my first marriage) advised me, 'Whatever you do Helen, go for surgery as quickly as you can. Don't hang around.' David's advice is reliable. The cancer is out of me today. I have another chance at life.

My new breast, which I find is called in hospital a flap, is made up of a three to four-inch section of skin from my tummy and other tissue, stitched up with a V underneath, keeping the skin on top, enough to match the right one. Part of a rib has had to be cut out in order to thread it all through, including veins. I have a new belly button, also an innie, created so my tummy looks like real. When a nipple is later tattooed on my new breast, I will feel it in my tummy, where the repositioned skin was before. They say the body doesn't lie, but it can get fooled.

It is about 6.30 p.m. and I can hear the nurses talking between themselves about me and my fellow inmates – sorry, patients. My hearing is eerily acute. They are going through each patient left in the recovery room in turn. Most have gone already, but there are still two left. I strain to hear what the male nurse is now saying.

'She's not doing well, she'll have to go back into theatre later. I'm just trying to track down an anaesthetist.'

The nurse has told me I am OK, that the operation went well, but now I am thinking he's just told me that to keep me quiet. I thought the other patient was a man, so by process of deduction the person who 'isn't doing well' must be me. Why am I still being held in the recovery room hours after the op? Scenes from my life literally start flashing before my eyes with my inner voice cursing me for taking the decision to have an eight-hour operation and not a simple mastectomy, which would have taken less than three hours. Stupid vanity. My children need me.

The phone rings and I can hear the clear, persistent, beautiful voice of my older daughter Unity at the other end, echoing my question.

'Why is my mum not on the ward yet?'

'We're still waiting for a porter. I'm sorry. I'll chase the ward again.' The nurse sounds tired, resigned to NHS cuts, overwork, underpay.

A porter finally comes and takes me to the plastic surgery ward. I never find out what happened to the other patient, who must have been a woman after all.

I need to let go of my distrust and focus on the reality of my future with the hand that life has dealt me. My two daughters and my friends have been amazing, tender and loving, organising a WhatsApp group to share photos of candles being lit on the day of my op to send me light and love.

Everyone on the ward is quiet: we need our strength to deal with the pain. Talking is more of an effort; endurance is what it takes. I will lie here for another four days before they take the tubes out and my skin has healed enough for me to get out of bed and walk again. While the body might be able to do it, my mind screams at me, 'No! You'll split open!'

My six-foot-two-inch son Will comes in to visit on the fourth day, with his big, easy grin creasing up his green eyes (like his grandfather's). He lights up the ward. 'Come on, Mum.' He is patient, encouraging.

My children give me strength: I can't let them down. As the Chinese proverb says, to get through the hardest journey we need take only one step at a time, but we must keep on stepping. The poet David Whyte also says, 'Start close in.' The first lines of the poem come back to me.

> *Start close in,*
> *don't take the second step*
> *or the third,*
> *start with the first*
> *thing*

> *close in,*
> *the step*
> *you don't want to take.*

Gingerly, I swing my legs down from the bed to place them on the pale floor. Instead of focussing on the pain, I look into my son's eyes.

The first is always the most difficult. Then another. I can do this.

Three days later, I am on the way back to my tiny flat in Flask Walk in Hampstead, above what used to be the pink Mystical Fairies shop and is now a sleek, chic beauty salon. I live here with my younger daughter, Lilly, who wanted to come to London with me to study for her A levels and be closer to her older sister. A good friend, Jill, has organised the journey back, and helps me leave hospital, having prepared the first meal home for me in advance. The Addison Lee taxi driver goes slowly, kindly, over the bumps, each surprisingly painful, ignoring the beeps and honks of the held-up drivers behind. Lilly and Unity are waiting to uplift me with their love and hugs and care. 'Welcome home, Mum.' I try not to burst into tears of gratitude.

•

The natural order of things. They say that, don't they, when they talk about a child dying before his or her mother, father, parents. 'It is against the natural order of things.' And when a child dies, even as a young man, it is hard for us as parents, siblings, humans, to bear. We know it is wrong and it shakes the foundations of our own lives. I am glad that my parents lived; they could have died too, from heartbreak. And through having my own family, my three children – a girl, then a boy, then another girl, the same shape of family that my mother would have had if my baby sister had survived – I have three wonderful beings on the planet to treasure. Amongst my mother's papers, I found a note which said that the time she spent looking after my children was the happiest time of her life. Time can heal, as they also say. Whoever they may be.

I have just seen a tweet from Matt Haig, celebrating the twentieth anniversary in May 2020 of him hitting rock bottom and stopping being suicidal.

'The main reason not to take your own life is because you aren't just taking your own life. You are taking the life of every future version of you that is grateful you stuck around. Brains evolve. Neuroplasticity is real. We become different people. Pain shifts. Life wins.'

•

By 2018, the day of my mother's funeral, my life has already changed so much. My divorce in 2014 was not easy, but I am lucky enough to remain close with members of my ex-husband's family. My other brother-in-law, Pete, told me firmly, 'You're always part of our family. You're tribe.'

I am so blessed with family, and friends, my tribe, that my cup brims over.

As well as my own children I have a wonderful man, Tim, two step-daughters, 'bonus daughters' as I like to call them, and a scruffy little dog, Bentley, so called because he is huge inside. There will be more friends and family here for my mother's funeral, for support.

I am a lawyer, with some books on divorce under my belt as a writer, and an academic textbook of which I am an editor. I have learned so much from my clients and the other practitioners I work with, every one. I have had the immense privilege of training lawyers to collaborate, to talk, to mediate, with a working partnership lasting for decades with the aptly named Suzy Power. I have more plans to come – I dare not even share with you how big those ambitions are. Oh, hold on. That won't work. I'll need to share those dreams with you, otherwise they may not come true. Talking always helps.

My life might have turned out very differently. My favoured approach – just keep putting one foot in front of the other, don't fall into the crater, don't even look up through hard times, just keep going – worked. But also, I have been lucky. What I really cannot express is how grateful I am for the times that I have now. And then things will change again. They always do.

Chapter 28

The White Envelope

Envelopes usually hide what is inside: a card, a letter, usually a bill, maybe even, although that's rare these days, a cheque. Good and bad news. My mother chose to write down her secrets on the outside of a white envelope which was already used, marked in ink *Private and Confidential*, but not by her.

The Thursday morning after she died, quite early, before I was due to go to work, I was sorting through some papers in the spare room – files I'd been working on – and noticed the envelope. It hadn't been on my mind. If you had asked me, before I fully read it, what I thought she might have been talking about, I'd have said that probably she was finally realising how self-absorbed she had been all her life, and she wanted to apologise.

If you're the daughter of a narcissistic mother, it's hard to let go of the hope that she will change, empathise – even if, logically, you should have abandoned that years ago, because she wasn't made that way, because, in turn, of something that happened to her in childhood. Hope was, is, hugely important to me. My younger daughter's middle name is Hope. But I had learned to let go of that particular expectation – let's call it that, rather than hope – through good, and longer-term, therapy in my fifties with Sue Lewis and with a group of women, all her clients, whom she organised to work together on a self-help basis. We call it the Phoenix Group. It's not that it was all about my mother – things are more complex than that, and my father had narcissistic traits too – but I needed to learn from other women with similar experiences what had happened to them, and to be able to say there things like 'I never felt I was good enough around my mother, I was worried everything was my responsibility, my fault,' and not have to see shock in another's face. We also monitor one another in a way to make sure that our own behaviour doesn't become too narcissistic; everyone is on the spectrum in one way or another. We still meet up, around three or four times a year, though all our parents have been dead for some time now.

On this Thursday morning, I decided to read all of the white envelope, although I had not read all the papers she had called her memoir. I still haven't. The bits I read are not always true, and are all about her. I've had enough of her in my head for now. Boundaries are my best friend.

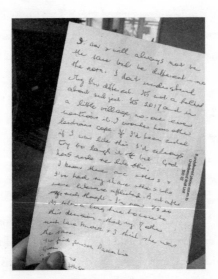

The white envelope

'I am and will always not be the same but be different – not the norm. I don't understand why I'm different. It's not a talked about subject. It's 2017 and in a little village no one ever mentions it. I wonder how other …'

Then I stumble at the next word. Hold on – what? What am I reading here?

'Tim, Tim!' I call out. 'Would you mind coming in here and having a look at this? Look. Right here. What do you think that word says?'

Tim looks at the envelope through his glasses, deciphering my mother's writing.

He looks at me and, after a pause, in his authoritative BBC voice, says, 'Lesbians.'

'Yes. That's what I thought it said.'

We both look at each other, shock dissolving into giggles. Oh dear. I don't think my mother would have expected us to laugh.

'Can you believe it?' I ask. 'I can't.'

Or can I? Things suddenly, in a rush, start to make more sense. Her secretiveness. The years before she married my father, which were never explained. The fact that my parents never hugged or held hands, unless there was a camera.

'Come on, then, carry on reading,' says Tim. 'You're better at her handwriting.' He hands back the envelope.

'I wonder how other lesbians cope. If I'd been asked if I was like this I'd always try to laugh it off but God has made me like this. I know there are others and I've had my share' – what? – 'I've had my share of others who were likewise afflicted.'

'Afflicted?' Oh God, my poor dear mum. 'Afflicted' is a terrible word.

'But after much thought – I'm now 85 so it's taken a long time to come to this decision – that my Mother must have known and I think she was the same.'

'Here we go,' I say. 'This is like the flipping *Titanic*. She's bringing everyone down with her, including Grannie.' I go back to reading to Tim.

'The first person – Pascaline. Gwen. Shirley – no. Margaret Johnson. Evelyn.'

'Gwen? Gwen? Right. Gwen. I'm going to email her right now.'

'Hang on a minute. What's on the other side of the envelope, Helen?'

I turn the envelope over, wondering when my mother wrote this. She mentions 2017, but she says she's eighty-five, so probably before her last birthday, on 27th November, when she was actually eighty-six. Unless that's the mild cognitive disorder too.

'And now all I have is a calmness, to try to get on with everyone and if they respond by being friendly that's all I ask for. So going back many years, my Mother used to tell me her father used to beat her mother until she died at an early age after she produced [my mother leaves a blank here – it was actually five] children and this affected her and she never recovered but never spoke of it either. For her it was a taboo subject. When my sister came along after 7 years of being an only one I was devastated and eventually I realised she wasn't as I was.'

And that's it. The envelope stops. I am so bored with this version of my mum's life, I tsk in irritation. Same old, same old. Blah. 'My sister came along and I was devastated. My mother wouldn't let me go to Uni-ver-si-ty.'

It was you, you who held yourself back Mum, not them. You could have studied at the Open University; you could have tried more with Judy. You could have talked. Ahh, that's it. It always comes back to the lack of talking. The silences. Well, no more of that now. But why did you wait until you died, before all of this came out? It's so typical.

'Isn't it sad, Helen, that she was never able to be with someone who would make her happy?' Tim asks.

'I'm not convinced anyone could make my mother happy, but yes. It is sad.'

'You know what, you haven't just got the book about David to write now. You'll have to write about this too, it's too extraordinary to let go, don't you think?'

Tim knows of the promise I made to myself; it was one of the things we'd talked about when we met online two years before. We found we were talking for so long, and so deeply, on the phone that we ended up wanting to talk together every day for the rest of our lives. He had nailed it for me by not just saying 'I want you' but also, 'Your happiness and wellbeing are the most important thing in the world to me right now.' What a gift.

'Trust my mother. Just at the point when I think all of it is over, that the coast is clear to talk about what really happened to David, she makes her own confession and trumps it.'

I call each of my children to tell them. They have similar responses, laughing, saying, 'That's so cool. We've got a gay grannie!' None of us had any inkling. My children have had a different experience of my mum. She was a devoted grannie. I wish she could have known how easy for us her coming out would be. But then again I can't begin to understand how terribly difficult she must have believed it was for her.

•

To tell the truth, I am not exactly impressed with my own reactions, and I don't expect you to be. I don't want to pretend that I dealt with it all brilliantly. I couldn't find advice – even online, where you can get advice about anything from other people who have been through the same thing, however weird. The input I had from other people sometimes raised even more questions. I told a gay partner at my firm of solicitors what had happened. She said, 'Do you think your parents had a lavender marriage?' I hadn't even heard of that.

I type into a search engine: 'How do you deal with a parent's posthumous confession they were gay?' There are few results and they are mostly to do with people finding out their child is gay or their parent is gay before they died. I tell my children about drawing this blank. My younger daughter says, 'Why did you put posthumous? If you put "after death" you might get somewhere, Mum.' She's right, but there's still nothing which specifically helps me.

I am going to email Gwen; I want to know more. But then what about Judy? Would she be able to cope with all this, now? Gwen is Judy's friend as well as Mum's. I can put that off for now; telling Judy before the funeral would create more drama and would simply not be kind. If I speak to Gwen, she will speak to Judy.

For once, I need to be patient. I'll hold off writing to Gwen until the funeral is over.

Chapter 29

Tim and I head into my black Peugeot to drive to my mum's flat in Waddesdon. He drives so that I can practise my eulogy: there's a sentence in it about David's death that I know I will stumble over. Some things never heal completely, and that's fine, because it is a part of me. It's also a part of who I am that I can allow myself to feel all the feelings. While I read through, I twist Mum's opal ring on my little finger. It comforts me, although part of that is the fact that I can choose when to have her with me and when to leave her behind in the jewellery box.

I don't want to catch Aunty Judy's eyes while I speak. I have already run this past my cousin Sue, Judy's daughter, seven years younger than her brother Ricky. The same gap as between each of our mothers. Patterns run like that in families, even birthdays sometimes fall on the same day.

'Well, Helen. Goodness. What a surprise. I really had no idea,' Sue says.

'Me neither. Makes me feel stupid, you know, like when there's a news story about a woman turning up at hospital with bad stomach pains and being told by the doctor that she's expecting a baby and it'll be born in the next hour.'

'Well, that's a bit dramatic,' Sue laughs. She laughs easily, like her mum. 'And I think you'd have spotted that. But I know what you mean.'

'Do you think it's OK not to tell your mum just yet? I think it will be a shock for her. It's like a double betrayal in a way.'

'It's your decision, Helen. I don't really know, there are things which cut both ways. Fifty-fifty, I'd say. It's up to you. And remember that your mum got everything she wanted.'

'That's true, I suppose. Although maybe not, it didn't last. Nothing does though.'

'Is Gwen not coming?'

'No, she says she's not well enough, and her wife Maud has been poorly too. Let's meet at the church, but I'll pop in to Mum's flat before the funeral. Your mum said she'd like a few more photos for her photo display at the wake, so she'll have those.'

'OK let's do that. Say ten o'clock at the church?'

'Cool beans,' I say, catching myself. It's a good thing I said that to Sue, who knows me. It's not on to show that my overwhelming emotion after Mum's death is relief.

Tim and I stop off at Mill Court. My parents had wanted to be near their grandchildren, as my two youngest attended Waddesdon School in the same village. And me, of course.

Tim stays in the car while I go in. The mouldy smell has not gone away.

I totter in on my black suede platform shoes. Damn, I'll have to take those off later. I look in the drawer under the bed where Mum kept her papers, remembering the times I searched for the (non-existent) documents to prove I wasn't from this family. There is a picture of my mother's friend, Margaret Johnson, in a daffodil-yellow trouser suit standing by the pillared gateposts in Slade Hooton, looking coquettishly at the camera with her head on one side. It sits next to a couple of photos of Gwen when she was much younger, maybe even at school? They are on top of an album of my brother's photos, ninety-nine of motocross bikes, one or two of David himself. And a brown envelope with a D scrawled on the top right-hand corner. I must remember to leave that in the car.

I scoop these up with the formal professional photos too, black and white, which my parents organised when I was four and David two. My mother was not wearing her opal ring when the photos of her were taken, just a set of pearls, three strands, and her wedding ring, with a rather formal dark tweed suit, her golden blond hair high in a swept-up bun. My father was also in a dark suit, looking dapper. David and I are dressed in jumpers knitted by our mother, mine with wooden toggles down the front. Outside the trees are bare, with the sunlight shining through.

I remember that David, aged two, did not want to have his photo taken and was crying. The photographer gave him a lens to play with: in one photo, David's attention has switched to the lens. My father's irritation is palpable, whereas my mother's look is one of relief. I'm just watching. The next shot is the one. The photographer gets it right: the dream family picture. We are all four smiling, two groups of two. I sit on my father's lap, us two darker, my brother on my mother's, both blond.

David's attempt to wriggle away has been distracted by the lens. We are all looking at the photographer. My father's smile practised and professional, my mother smiling more with her lips and less with her eyes. I look more worried, observing what is going on. My and my brother's hair partings determinedly follow our father's, on the right. He was always combing our hair, giving us a parting just like his.

Underneath these photos are lots of my mother as a little girl: long, white-blond hair flowing in the wind, or neatly plaited, with a huge, happy smile in all of them. Mum really does look happier in the years before her sister was born.

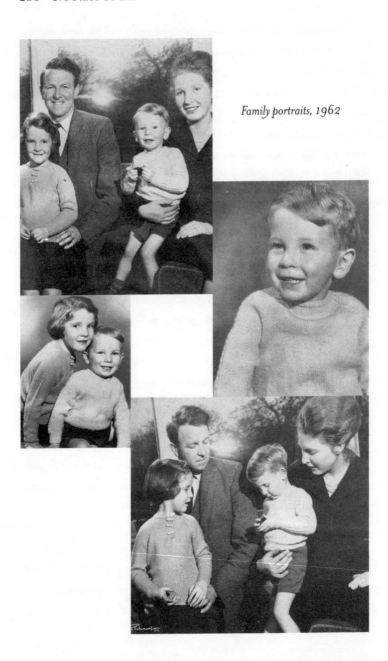

Family portraits, 1962

I pop into the Five Arrows where the wake will be held and add these to Judy's photo display, titled by her, with foresight, 'My Sister: The Enigma'.

Perhaps we all knew in a way.

•

My mother's eulogy is prepared; all I now have to do is say it. The music for the funeral will start with Samuel Barber's *Adagio for Strings* and end with George Harrison's 'Give Me Love (Give Me Peace on Earth)', George Harrison being her favourite Beatle. The peace on earth bit might in truth be more for the listeners than my mum. My Fitbit tells me I am doing a cardiac workout, and my heart will race fastest of all when I speak. There are my children smiling through tears, their partners, there is Tim in the church, the feel of his hand on my back a recent, comforting memory. Aunty Judy, don't look, Sue, Ricky, the rest of my family and friends. They are all willing me on to do this, to pay tribute to the first love of my life. There will be things I don't say, but I need to put my best foot forward.

Everyone carries more than they usually let on and sometimes the burdens are far heavier than we know; it's one of the reasons why we need to be kind with ourselves and others. If I hadn't known that before I was a family lawyer and mediator for thirty years, I know it now.

As I speak, holding my notes in both hands, heart racing, her opal ring seems to flash more red than anything, and I catch myself worrying that my mother might be cross with me.

Chapter 30

My Thanksgiving Service Eulogy for Mum

'I am and will always not be the same but be different.'

My mother's words – which I found when looking through the papers she had brought with her to the care home she spent just eight days in towards the end of her life, before a peaceful – and quick – passing.

Papers – writing – were important to her. For Christmas 2016 she prepared a recipe book for each of her beloved grandchildren, Unity, Will and Lilly, with recipes and tips for every day of the year. In addition to long, complex recipes for Stuffed Chicken in Pastry with Braised Chicory, for example, she gives the cook Saturdays off and allows standards to be lowered. For Saturday the thirteenth of January, for example, her direction is: 'Pizza. If you live in a town send out for one. If not, buy one.'

On the day before she died, I had visited her with my partner Tim and had read over to her some of the Christmas messages and cards she received last year. She had a dauntingly lengthy Christmas card list and faithfully sent out cards and messages to her friends and family including hundreds of messages by email. She was a silver surfer. 'I find writing letters soothing,' she told me.

So, this is a tribute to my mother, Monica Burnett Garlick, also known in the family as Pip, because she was the apple of her daddy's eye. Born in Doncaster, she was the oldest daughter of Marjorie and Lesley Nicholson. Her mother was a teacher who had gone to Sheffield university and studied French and spent a year at the Sorbonne, and her father worked on the railways, but was also a part-time magician.

Mum had apparently been told by her parents that she was the only one, so when her sister Judy arrived seven years later, it was something of a surprise. Mum lived through the Second World War with her parents and her sister Judy, and the family settled to live at Palace Farm, Scrooby, an idyllic house with a lovely garden and a kitchen which always seemed to smell of toasted Hovis and freshly boiled sheets (at least that's how I remembered it).

Pip, aged 4

Mum left school at fifteen, trained as a secretary and went out to work. When she was working for George Garlick (my grandfather – so you can probably guess what is coming) his youngest son Geoffrey, back from studying at Cambridge, used to come and revise at the office in the holidays. My aunt Judy, Mum's sister, saw their first meeting – they both blushed furiously and that was it.

My mum was a beauty with corn-gold hair and blue eyes. She married at twenty-three. After my father qualified as a solicitor, he set up a brass plaque for his firm G C Garlick & Co. in Doncaster. She worked for him, pregnant with me, typing pretend letters initially when people came into the office, however the practice flourished and became a big part of their lives, Dad running his office in Doncaster and Mum running the Sheffield office after she returned to work. They were married for fifty-nine years until his death in July 2014.

*My parents' wedding, 1st October 1955. Aunty Judy, first left; Uncle Jimmy,
third left; my grandfather Les, second right*

They had two children, me and my brother David, two years younger.
Mum also later suffered a miscarriage, which I imagine also had an
effect on her.

Their lives were decidedly different, extra-ordinary. They moved
house eleven times in sixteen years and went from a terraced house in
Doncaster to Slade Hooton Hall, an eight-bedroomed William and
Mary house via various properties, including our much-loved family
home at Leahurst in Tickhill. My father used to quote Mark Twain:
'Buy land, they're not making it anymore'. At one time they had at
least five properties, including the Salt Box, the family's holiday home
in Marhamchurch in Cornwall, a flat in Bow in London, a cottage in
Litton in Derbyshire, and their Spanish villa.

My mother gamely ran all these different houses on a tight budget.
She had been given a Snoopy apron one Christmas saying 'Home is
where the supper dish is', which summed up their rolling-stone life-

style. Mum was a remarkable cook, having gone on a cordon bleu course and would give tips, like always make sure you have a bit of red in every meal.

They used to throw extraordinary parties, in my father's role as President of the Doncaster and District Law Society and President of the Yorkshire Union of Law Societies, with enormous quantities of sherry trifle, made in washing-up bowls. My grandfather, her father, in charge of opening the wine, used to sometimes pop the odd champagne cork in some rather extraordinary directions, notably some large rear ends. Bottoms up! They loved parties.

Mum and Dad also were invited, twice, to the Queen's garden parties at Buckingham Palace. Mum was fairly convinced that this was because she had been a Girl Guide commissioner, Dad because he had been President of the Yorkshire Union of Law Societies for thirty-seven years. Whatever the reason, they got to meet the Queen and the Queen Mother. Who greeted them by saying, 'How very nice to see you. Again.' That's probably not the first time some people here have heard that story. My dad did not shirk from telling a good story several times. Sometimes several hundred times. At least that's how I remembered it.

They also loved the sun and travel. It is probably no coincidence that my mother died on the twenty-first of December, the shortest day of the year, when the sun is furthest away.

They travelled widely: to China, Japan, Africa and America as well as Europe, going away for a month at least once a year on a long-haul trip, and latterly also on various cruises. They also loved the theatre, concerts and the cinema and would often take in four shows in a weekend trip to London. My mother especially loved the Proms.

I talked to Christopher Henderson last week, a childhood friend of my brother's in Slade Hooton, who recalled playing Ivanhoe in the garden of Slade Hooton Hall and what a privilege (his word) it was to visit. 'Your parents were liberal and cultured. They let us watch *Monty Python* and *Top of the Pops* – my parents said they were rubbish and insisted on turning the telly off – and would even talk about people like David Bowie.' They were generous-hearted, and welcomed having people to stay, including friends of mine and my brother's, and were a big part of their lives as well as the lives of their many friends.

An anomaly in all of this was that my mother, as she told me, was happiest on her own. If she was a book, it would have been hard to read her. Part of what she kept most private was the loss of her son, my blue-eyed, fair-haired brother David, when he was nearly twenty-one, whom she idolised (her word). David took his life when I was away in America for three months.

His death ripped a void into me and I can barely conceive what it was like for my mother. To lose a child must be one of the greatest tortures on earth – I cannot imagine getting through one minute if one of my children were to die, never mind the thirty-six-plus years she endured. Each person's pathway through grief is unique. Her way was to bury what had happened. Her grief was immense and hidden. It is a heavy burden to keep a secret for such a long time.

She found solace in travel, in her long-standing and loyal friends, in her continuing curiosity in the world, in her faith, in her reading. She taught me to read when I was three. She also – very importantly – taught me to follow my own path. I was something of a rebel at school and on one occasion received a school report, saying 'Helen is too independently minded'. My father was telling me off at the table, when my mother stood up, crying 'No, you're wrong. She has to be that. It's her independent spirit that will get her through life.'

She was a loyal mother. I did not doubt that she loved me, even if she might have sometimes found it hard to be demonstrative.

She and my father supported me and my family as much as they could. When we had happy times, they loved sharing those. When we had a very difficult time when my former husband was very ill, they gave us very practical and much-needed help financially. My mum helped us campaign alongside John Bercow against the waste incinerator locally and HS2, delivering leaflets, telling people what she thought.

She had strong views.

I have kept what she also chiefly treasured to the last. She doted on her grandchildren, looking after Unity and then Will two days a week when they were little in London, and moving to Waddesdon to be close to the family. For her birthday in 2016, we took her up to the Shard (a long-held ambition) for a birthday meal. Last October, as a family, we visited Cornwall to see my brother's grave where my father's ashes are also buried, and where hers will be too. She saw the sea, a little bit of sun, went to the Eden Project, we cooked, played Scrabble and Monopoly. Their grave will be inscribed with Cardinal Newman's words, 'Peace at the last'.

Thank you for coming. I wish you peace and light, Mum. And sunshine.

●

The funeral passes well. It is a crisp, sunny day, as my mum would have wanted. There is a good turnout, maybe sixty people plus. Not bad when so many of my parents' friends have died or are too ill to come. The Five Arrows in Waddesdon is a beautiful setting, which my mother (and father) loved. It glitters gold and black, a Rothschild version of a pub. Many of the guests now are vegetarian or vegan: fewer pigs died for this repast.

Before the funeral I spoke on the phone to one of David's friends from Slade Hooton, Christopher. He wouldn't be able to come. 'I'm sorry I can't be there. They were so generous to me, taking me to Cornwall. Slade Hooton Hall was like a second home.'

He mentioned a few unexpected things in our phone call. First, he recalled how he and David used to practise on his air rifle. 'One of us would hold up targets, like bulls eyes, at arm's length and the other would fire at the target for practice. We'd take it in turns.'

'Good grief that sounds dangerous,' I said, my older-sister instinct coming into play.

Christopher laughed before he paused, then told me, hesitantly, that David once told him that he did not want to live after he was twenty.

'I never told anyone that before. He was about twelve when he said it, and he was quite certain. He hated the thought of getting old.'

'I'm so sorry you've had to carry that,' I say.

'I also remember that David hated pooing. It was weird,' Christopher said.

'Yes, it is. And, yes, he was like that. I'd completely forgotten.'

I'm glad Christopher told me these things. It made sense in a way: another few pieces of the jigsaw I was building so that I would know better what had happened and figure out, maybe, why.

As we are saying goodbyes after the wake I catch up with Evelyn, my parents' old friend, and tell her a little of what I know already. She suggests we meet up.

'Homosexuality is a complicated thing,' she said. 'Let's talk about it more in future if you like. Coffee? Lunch? Not now, not here.'

Chapter 31

Following the funeral, I needed to talk to Aunty Judy, which I did as soon as I could. Once I'd spoken with her (she forgave me; agreed it was best I hadn't told her beforehand), we both got in touch with Gwen, about the relationship between her and my mum, which started when Gwen, aged thirteen, went to Judy's twelfth birthday party. My mother was nineteen.

Judy and I both suspected that maybe other people later on knew and we were kept out of the loop, but as it turns out, we think, no one else knew except a tight inner circle.

Given our ignorance, I'll hand over to Gwen now to explain more about what happened from her emails to me and my aunt. There are a couple of emails from me too.

22nd January 2018

Hello Gwen and many thanks indeed for your email. Yes – am glad that you have opted for a donation. Thank you so much. The florists in Bicester are not great. And flowers will come and go …

Have sent you the draft orders of service – I hope that's OK and not too intrusive?

Will be in touch after 30th January if not before – there are a couple of things Mum raised in her papers which I'd like to talk to you about but would rather this was after 30th if possible.

Hope things are OK with you.

Much love,

Helen xx

23rd January 2018

Dear Helen,

Thanks for sending me the details of the funeral and memorial services. Ten out of ten for your chosen hymns and music.

The hymns I know very well and like. Maybe you knew this but Pip and I used to go to the same piano teacher in Avenue Road in Doncaster – Gwen Miles. Pip used to play the Moonlight Sonata along with a lot of Chopin, and the Holst Planets Suite was the first piece of music that Pip ever recommended to me. Adagio for Strings is a lovely piece of music and very well known to me; your father once sold me an LP record of this when I said how much I liked it for 10 shillings, pre-decimal.

So very well done and I so much wish I could be there to share it all with you – however painful and sad a time it may be. I will certainly be with you in spirit.

I don't think I have any photos that I can add to your collection as mine are very old and some of them the same as Judy has. The one taken on the beach in France Pip sent to me herself when she came home.

Please ring me whenever you like regarding what you want to know and I hope I can supply you with the answers you need.

With love,

Gwen xx

I spoke with Gwen on the phone, who confirmed that everything my mother said was true. She said she had been waiting nearly all her life for a phone call about this. I agree to send her a copy of the envelope. The rest of the emails all post-date Mum's funeral.

My dear Helen,

Only just read this – went to bed early.

Thanks very much, can't read the letters until I enlarge them on my computer but I have always known this about Pip. I'm just sorry she didn't tell anyone else whilst she was alive.

More later, asap when I've read the letter.

Much love to you,

Gwen xx

•

Hello again Helen, I meant to say I agree with you that telling Judy about your Mum's orientation would certainly help her understand why she never fully understood her before.

Also it would make me feel happier because I've always felt as though I was hiding something from Judy and I haven't really liked doing that.

As Pip chose to tell you now, I would be able to be truthful when she asks me questions.

Not long now to your hols. I would be counting the hours if I were in your shoes.

Much love again,

Gwen xx

•

Dear Jude,

Thanks for your e-mail. I can understand why you feel you can't talk about it yet perfectly, and I'd just like to say how I have started to feel about the whole subject. The reason I was going to talk to you today was because I want it all over and done with because frankly it's not doing me any good at all. I thought I could cope with this and I was glad in one way that this had all come out.

As you know I've had an awful lot of illness, strife and stress over the past 2 years and have now come to the point where I actually can't cope with any more. My own delving back into the past and possibly some of the unhappiness connected with that isn't a good thing.

I always maintained my friendship with Pip as you know and was faithful in keeping her secret. We were good friends and yes, I did love her as a friend until the day she died and shall continue to do so within my own head. I did tell [Maud] as I couldn't enter my future life with her on a secret past.

However, I find that I am, inordinately, cross with Pip for freeing up her own mind with her revelation and upsetting you and Helen to the extent that it has. Not unsurprisingly I must say.

I have nothing to say about my own relationship with Pip except what you already know about my meeting with her at your birthday party and our subsequent gay relationship (until she married and not after). I thought you may remember how your Mum got a bee in her bonnet and thought I was the one who had lured Pip into 'dirty deeds' (her words not mine) and told her she either got married or got out.

Pip always intended to get married I think as that was the life she wanted, she wanted the lifestyle, the position in society, the money, travel, children, the lot. This was her choice. In those days it was very, very difficult for gay people and especially for men (who were criminalised because of it). I know quite a few respectable men in public life who married because it was the right thing to do and we have at least 3 female friends who were previously married with children. The women we know, once they accepted they had made a wrong choice and one they couldn't spend the rest of their lives with, did divorce the husbands after their children had grown up and changed their life to where they felt more comfortable.

I think Pip did love Geoffrey when she married him, she even asked me 'did I know how to get him to propose to her'!

I honestly don't know whether Geoffrey did know she was a lesbian beneath it all, as I've said before to Helen maybe she was bi-sexual although I always see that as wanting the best of both worlds and a bit of a cop out.

The only person I know of whom Pip did really care for was Margaret Johnson (I nursed her when I was a Ward Sister in Doncaster) and possibly Shirley to some extent when she was at school. There were many other women whom she had associations with over the years but I don't somehow feel they were serious, or she would have told me. Evelyn whom they rented out their Bow flat to for a year she made advances towards but they were not reciprocated.

Many colleagues or friends I introduced her to she 'befriended' though some of them I think just for who they were, you may remember (forgotten her first name now) Surname Dr [████████] (a female doctor at the DRI). I'm not sure if Helen didn't go and stay with her. But she wasn't gay I'm fairly sure.

Anyway no doubt I shall forgive Pip for her revelations soon, it would be silly not to, but just now I must get it all out of my head and think of myself first and of Maud too, as she doesn't like seeing me upset and not well physically. We both need a rest from stress.

So I understand when you say you need a few days Jude but I can't afford any more days I'm afraid – I have been aware that this was on the cards for some weeks now when Helen first told me she wanted to ask me something that she had come across in Pip's papers so with me I have been wondering what sort of mess Pip had left which may entail questions being asked of me. She must have known I'd be the one person left alive who could answer them.

I don't want this to make any difference to our friendship Jude, or mine with Helen but I just had to say this now and not leave it any longer. I may send a copy of this letter to Helen as it will help her regarding her father.

Just send me a brief reply saying you understand why I have had to write this.

Love Gwen xx

•

Dear Helen,

Thanks for yours and you're very nearly right in all you say.

I'm sorry I maybe appeared to criticise your Mum because in my book no one should ever be allowed to do that apart from the daughters themselves because it's their own Mum and had anyone done so with mine I would have bitten their head off.

I know I'm irrational at the moment, I know that I personally didn't ever see Pip as predatory and I would never, ever put my own sexual orientation down to her. I know I was young but in my head I was far older than my actual years.

Apart from that I believe that everyone is responsible for their own actions, even in extenuating circumstances. I always have thought this although it may sound a little rigid.

You're right in that I have tried to circumvent, somehow, my grieving for Pip by trying not to think about it properly. I'd been so absolutely devastated by my losses and near loss plus continued and worsening physical health that I was determined to 'keep this under control' – a mistake obviously, smart of you to see this.

Regarding your Mum's dementia – I realise what you say is correct as well. Maud has said this to me a lot this last few weeks and having had to see my sister's changes over 6 years with a similar illness then I'd be thick not to understand. Not to mention my knowledge of Nursing.

You did send me the tribute and thought it very well phrased, I liked it, so thank you.

I sure I will be able to move forward now and everything will move back into a sensible and rational place. I do hope both you and Jude manage the same.

With love,

Gwen xx

•

My dear Gwen,

Thank you for all your frankness – it does help (I think) to find out more what has been kept so hidden for a long time. Judy and I have been sharing things. We are both pretty open and it is so weird on the one hand to realise how many secrets were kept – on the other things are sort of falling into place more. One thing I keep wondering about is how much my father knew? If you could help elucidate that I would be very grateful.

With love,

Helen xx

•

Dear Helen,

Your e mail came through a bit mixed up with a page full of computer mailing information which I didn't understand. It's something to do with virus checking I think but reads like gobbledegook.

Anyway I was able to read the main question. I don't know if Geoffrey ever guessed, surely he must have. But I really don't know.

Margaret Johnson (who was not just a passing flirtation) used to stay at your house regularly and once said to me that she found it very hard sleeping in the next bedroom to your parents. I know Slade Hooton Hall had thick walls so maybe it was her imagination running riot.

I think your mum genuinely cared for Margaret J but later on when she visited Maud and I in 1975 in Sheffield she (your Mum) denied she was gay. People were very closeted in those days and it wasn't always easy to be truthful. But at least with women it wasn't an offence thank goodness.

I had been a Ward Sister in Doncaster and nursed Margaret Johnson and she was the biggest flirt I've ever met both with men and women. I don't know what help that is to you so I even wonder why I mention it. I think I'm just trying to console you.

I once went to the theatre with Geoffrey, he asked me to go as I think he said someone else had cancelled. Anyway the subject of the play (can't remember the name of it now) was a married woman having a lesbian affair. I was acutely embarrassed when I realised what it was about and often wondered what he knew and about whom.

Sorry to have no definite knowledge on this for you.

I'm sorry it's been such a shock for you both.

Much love, Gwen xx

Gwen died six months after my mother, again unexpectedly, after her own massive heart attack. Her funeral was arranged for two days after I married Tim, when I was on our honeymoon. Judy went, on behalf of the family.

Much later, in 2020, Tim and I watch a Netflix film, *A Secret Love*, a touching documentary about two North American women in their eighties who finally came out to their families, and about the love between them. It is immensely moving. The part where they show their love letters with all the bottoms torn off to hide their signatures, I found desperately sad.

I turn the idea over in my mind: might my mother, Pip, ever have lived a life like this, a life in which she loved and was loved by another woman and could live freely? Frankly it seems to me like sentimental tosh. My mum adored the lifestyle she had with my father and would not have given that up lightly, if at all. She had it all, as my cousin Sue rightly said, although losing my brother by his own hand must have been the worst torment in the world. Perhaps she felt it was her punishment.

Chapter 32

A few weeks after the funeral, I meet up with Evelyn. We'd agreed to meet in town, settling on lunch. I booked Cigala, a Spanish restaurant around the corner from work. I hoped that tapas and memories of sun and the Mediterranean would make our conversation easier.

She was a bit late. I remembered Evelyn as a career woman, businesslike, affable, kind, a little reserved, with bright, dark eyes, long eyelashes and a smile which lit up and transformed her face.

'I had forgotten where Lamb's Conduit Street was – is. I ended up being around Shaftesbury Avenue looking in all the wrong places,' she says, when she arrives.

That's a surprise. Everyone has Google Maps on their smartphones, don't they? But sometimes there are events which might pull down the carefully constructed walls of our existence; times when hidden things, things we've kept away from sight, are going to be exposed. There is an inevitability to a truth spilling out, demanding to be given words, unstoppable. A tipping point is reached. And that can be unnerving.

I understand Evelyn's nerves. I have something like that going on too, in the pit of my stomach. My heart is racing, as it has been so much over the last few weeks.

Here in front of me is a woman who is named on my mother's list of women she has had, or may have had, a relationship with. Is this woman, this diminutive, albeit sprightly woman, younger than my parents, who carefully looks after her appearance, another of my mother's lovers? Gwen – Judy and I had decided – might be prone to dramatics. Evelyn, I feel, will be a more reliable witness. Even though we all kind of want to be the heroes in our own stories, which means the 'truth' is always rather distorted, I sort of trust that Evelyn will tell me a version nearer to what might pass for the truth.

I smile and try to put her at her ease. We talk of my forthcoming move with Tim to Sussex, our new home with a wonderful view, and I tell Evelyn about how John Betjeman suggested the most important view of a house was from the inside out rather than looking at the house itself. I chatter about wedding plans (how my wedding music will start with Jackie Lee's 'On White Horses', my favourite song), holidays, my children. All of these are lovely things, though finding out about my mother's deception has made me question deep down whether I can ever really trust, or love, or form a relationship.

People say they love me. Actually, quite a lot of people over the years have said that they love me, but my experience is that they had a limited conception of what it is to love. And probably so do I. I have learned to be more wary, although Tim and I are still taking the leap of faith which is marriage.

I look at Evelyn in Cigala, frankly like an aeroplane pilot eyeing up where I might land, touch on the ground that we – I – might want to really talk about. After years of being a family mediator, the territory I now know well is the emotional landscape of a breakdown of trust; of hurt, disappointment, pain, all the feelings. I even have a list of feelings on my laptop these days, to broaden my knowledge beyond the go-tos of anger, grief, depression. I've needed to work at this and find out through experience – the wheel of fire as one colleague termed it – the need for exquisite sensitivity, patience, choice of language and gentleness to get to the heart, where work can be done to mend things. It takes time for people to reveal things. Sometimes – often – bravery.

I aim to give signals to Evelyn that it will be OK if she tells me stuff. I say, 'There have been so many years since my brother died, I can barely remember what things were like before then. Mum's grief after David died was immense. Dad's of course, too. It was hard to talk about and it was hard to talk to her. But thank you for coming today.'

I tell her that it is not so much the fact that my mother was gay, but her deception that had rocked me. I thought I had a reasonably tuned gaydar and that I could spot when secrets are not being said. I thought (actually do still think) that I can read an emotional land-scape and read the dynamics of what is going on. But I had no idea, not even an inkling, that my mother was gay. I tell her how open-minded my children are and that Mum would, we thought, have had an open and receptive audience if she had decided to share her sexual orientation. I tell her that as a family lawyer I've had many clients who decided that they were gay, sometimes after being married for years, especially since the Civil Partnership Act of 2005 gave a governmental nod of approval to gay relationships.

I tell her that I did find it shocking that my mother had been nine-teen when she initiated a relationship with Gwen, six years younger than her. Change the sexes of the participants – albeit willing partic-ipants as Gwen had stressed to me – to both of them being male, or an older male and a young girl, and it seems perhaps more shocking. Why would I think that? Is it a throwback to Queen Victoria's alleged refusal to believe that women could have sex together? Does a lack of physical male penetration make it more OK?

I tell her also that I would rather know the truth than be left with more secrets. At this, Evelyn lets out a breath. A sigh: maybe this is something of a relief for her, too?

She tells me facts, her story, chronologically. It is a way of ordering or marshalling what went on, which turns out to have more twists.

Evelyn was originally from Leeds. She successfully applied for a job in Sheffield but she knew few people. Evelyn knew she must start afresh. She met Gwen who suggested that she might like to meet Monica, my mother, whom she thought Evelyn might get on with.

Evelyn assures me that she was not gay, at least not then. 'At that time, I liked men, went out with men. I really wanted to get married and have children.' She tells a funny story of a short, bald-headed, rugby-playing farmer who took her out a few times and then proposed. 'You'll want for nothing. I'm a farmer. I'm rich and I'll give you anything you want. Just don't expect me to be faithful.' Evelyn recounts that she just burst out laughing and the farmer scarpered.

I know that nowadays she lives with a woman friend. I think they might be partners but I don't ask. Evelyn talks about her a lot. 'Mentionitis', my god-daughter Alex has termed it. The act of frequently talking about someone whom one loves. However, I really don't know and it is not my business.

But let's go back to Evelyn's, then recent, move from Leeds. She met up with my mother who then asked her out for dinner alone on a Friday night, at a steak house. My mother talked about how she had lived in London with another woman before her mother, my grandmother, came to London to insist that she came back up North and get married.

Evelyn says, 'Your mother could have told her [my grandmother] no. She was earning, she had her own life. But she presented this like being a martyr. I'm afraid that your mother could be quite,' she hesitates, 'manipulative.'

My turn now to breathe out more deeply. My mother could indeed be manipulative. It is sustaining to hear another woman of the same generation, sometimes termed 'the silent generation', say that.

Labelling a feeling, a problem, a trait, correctly, takes away some of its sting and gives a handle for it. It is words, not silence, that heal.

More dinner invitations from my parents followed, Evelyn explains. I can feel a 'but' coming on.

'But I just didn't really understand what was going on. She made a pass at me. Your mother would start to talk about things but then clam up. She was often quiet. I think she used that as a sort of strategy. She was quite closed, you know.'

I know, I nod, about her being closed. I finally pluck up courage to ask the question which has been on my mind from the start of this lunch.

'Did my father know?' I ask. 'Honestly, that's one thing that has been torturing me.'

Evelyn makes an understanding face. She is kind. I appreciate her empathy.

'I think he must have done. Eventually, after we'd met for a few weeks, your mother invited me to dinner at Slade Hooton Hall. Your father could barely bring himself to be civil to me when we first met. He was sort of angry. Maybe jealous? Far from the genial host I eventually knew him to be.' She looks into the distance for a while, then turns back to face me. 'I was, you know, very fond of Geoffrey.'

She has said that before and I had never really noticed. I notice now. She tells me that she and Granville – a gay, male friend of my parents – fell into a pattern where they would go to Slade Hooton Hall for Friday evening. My parents invited other guests, often clients. 'I think Granville and I were their only friends at those evenings. And there was a lot of drinking going on. Your parents both used to drink. Too much. It worried me.'

Granville told Evelyn about other women my mother had made passes at. Evelyn continues her story of the goings-on in Slade

Hooton, my teenage family home. 'I never really saw anything going on, but then I wasn't aware of much. Granville told me more.'

Evelyn made it clear to my mother that she was not interested. Then, after a month or so, my mother tried another tack.

'Monica told me that Geoffrey was in love with me and said she wanted me to have an affair with him.'

She searches my face for any sign of my reaction. I have learned over the years to put on a mediator's mask; look neutral. My outward expression is the mediator's face. I hope I give nothing away. She looks a bit more reassured.

'I've been thinking this morning, worrying over whether I should tell you this.'

'I'm glad you did,' I say, although I am so cut off from my own responses I really can't read myself today, never mind anyone else.

Evelyn continues. 'I really didn't know what to think when she asked me that.'

Her answer now leaves me with a number of other questions. Her saying that she 'did not know what to think' when my mother presented my father on a plate to her – did that mean that she was tempted? Mine is his child's response, and as a child I would rather that my father did not have affairs. But maybe if he had found happiness with someone else – would that not have been better? We talk about my mother.

'Your mother was not a happy woman,' Evelyn says. 'It seemed like she had everything. The status, the travel, children, the big house, several houses. But she used to complain about your father being grumpy. He needed an audience. He wouldn't have been able to cope without her. He was totally impractical.' I agree. He never could boil an egg.

'Their relationship was complicated.' We touch on that some more. How I cannot remember my parents saying they loved each other. About her distaste over my father in his demented years, refusing outside help, ending up being so stressed that she had psychotic episodes annually, always on 11th December. Another mysterious thing about my mother.

'But she did really love you,' Evelyn said. 'Her children were everything to her. You and David.'

'I didn't really experience that.' I say quietly. 'I feel I have something empty inside where I think other people feel filled up, happy and warm. I knew something didn't make sense.'

I mention to Evelyn a boyfriend I had who was at Cambridge, who came to stay at the house once. Evelyn casts back in her memory.

'I remember that your father said you had a Jewish boyfriend,' Evelyn recalls. 'Did he live in Pinner?'

'Nearly right,' I say. 'But it was Hatch End. I used to love his family. His sister was gay. He said two plus two might make plus seven or minus four in my family. I didn't understand what he was saying then. It was so confusing being in the middle of it all.'

We are both, rather suddenly, starting to tire. The nervous, adrenalin energy melts away and I feel sapped. I know I have to go back to the office soon to see a client and so pay the bill, refusing Evelyn's offer. She has actually gifted me so much.

●

When I later spoke to my older daughter about this, she said, 'You might want to think about boundarying this, Mum. It might be too much. It's of course up to you.'

I didn't make any more enquiries, more content now to let sleeping dogs lie. But perhaps my unconscious isn't?

I have a recurring dream in which my father has remarried an older woman, bookish with glasses, not as pretty as Evelyn. I keep finding this non-existent stepmother in my dreams in unexpected places. I go to make up a bed and she is already in it, thin, breathing quietly so I don't see her until I pull off the bedclothes. Or I'm walking along the beach and there she is, on the sea front. And then the dreams go away, just as they came.

Peace at the last, are the words which will go on my parents' gravestone, alongside my brother. But before I let this go and achieve some semblance of peace myself (I won't use the word closure, it's hackneyed, and anyway what does it mean? I prefer peace), I need to answer questions about what happened to my brother in February 1981.

Gravestone in the churchyard at St Marwenne's,
Marhamchurch 2017

Chapter 33

The Brown Envelope

I had put the rest of my mother's things in our garage, to sort out one day, apart from the plastic bag of jewellery and her opal ring, which of course I keep inside. Much of her stuff the children eventually looked through and took a few things for themselves: the musty smell did not make them appealing.

On the left-hand side of our garage are metal storage shelves, useful to keep things tidied away. Amongst unloved and probably now unusable tins of paint, almost empty screenwash containers, light bulbs waiting for a decision to be made as to whether they head to heaven in the recycling bin, I placed the brown envelope after I brought it back from Waddesdon, somehow not wanting it to be inside our Sussex home. It does not look old, preserved by lying in a drawer underneath the bed, protected from the light. It lay unseen by me for around thirty-six years. During that time, it was probably only seen by my parents.

The typed address on the envelope is my father's old office at number 6 Waterdale, Doncaster. The envelope has a large capital D scrawled in pencil on the top right-hand corner in my mother's distinctive handwriting. A bold, round, sweep of a curve, with a relatively short line downwards, which don't join up together. I know the D means David.

I felt I had to leave it there until I had enough time, internal space and perspective to take a look. I am not even sure if I want to, but is there any point in avoiding these truths?

The brown envelope

Pulling the papers out of the envelope, I see one bundle sewn up with green ribbon on the left-hand side, tightly stretched through five holes, the two ends of the ribbon sealed together with a red court seal. These are the legal documents relating to the court case to contest the first inquest verdict.

The bundle is headed:

IN THE HIGH COURT OF JUSTICE

QUEENS BENCH DIVISION

DIVISIONAL COURT

IN THE MATTER OF AN INQUEST

TOUCHING THE DEATH OF DAVID NICHOLAS GARLICK

   - and -

IN THE MATTER OF THE CORONERS ACT 1887

- and -

IN THE MATTER OF THE CORONERS (AMENDMENT) ACT
1926

The word 'touching' is a surprise, almost an emotion amongst legal papers. One page sticks out, it is bigger than the rest and has had to be folded into the bundle. It is a photocopy of a report in the *Sheffield Star* of April 25th 1981, four days after my birthday, not that that mattered. The headline (there are no pictures) is

SHOTGUN SUICIDE
Solicitor's son, 20,
died in country hall

I have to stop, give myself a break, hours or days, sometimes longer, before I can read everything. The papers include the witness statements here in Chapters 11 and 18, the newspaper reporter's notes, the letter from Reverend Jem Parsons and the pathologist's report. I know that I must have seen something of these papers before because I was caught up in the process of challenging the first inquest verdict but, perhaps like other things in my childhood, I had learned, without knowing I even did it, to dissociate. I confess I did not fully read the papers at that time, a terrible mistake for a lawyer, although for a human it was a protective strategy.

The three facts striking me now, which I did not know back in 1981, are:

My brother had himself bought this gun, a cheap, 'entry level', single barrelled Russian shotgun, for £46 (I don't know where he got that money from, a significant sum for him).

The cabinet left open that my father had referred to, which I had thought was a gun cabinet, was in fact a filing cabinet belonging to the owner of Bothamsall Hall. My brother must have looked through the filing cabinet, found the shotgun certificate, and altered the date of birth to make the holder nearer twenty-five than thirty-five (David could have carried this off. He looked older than his years).

My father was trying to present a case that my brother was happier than I knew him to be and that the gun had been bought for leisure purposes: rough shooting, as it was termed in the papers. He – my father – also told the police that my car and my dog belonged to David: an attempt to portray his life as more solid and secure than it was? In one line in his affidavit (for which he would have sworn the truth of its contents) my father states: 'The Affidavit of [Reverend Jeremy Parsons] which is herewith confirms that a few days before his death my son seemed happy, relaxed and cheerful. I verily believe that to have been his state of mind.' Those last two sentences hit me hard. Dad was adamant that my brother was in good spirits. But saying a thing really does not make it so.

I also force myself to look up what happens to a body after death, realising that the coroner might have tried to do a kindness to our family in determining that my brother died only the day before my father found him. His death, I discovered, could have been two or three days before, even more. Given David's character and the carefulness of his preparation, I believe that my brother would not have left anything to a chance earlier visit by my parents and that he would have completed his suicide before he knew they would arrive back in England, on Friday February 27th 1981. Awful, chilling, to realise that more likely than not my brother had been lying there dead for days, not hours, before my father found him.

There are two last facts which stay with me from the papers; maybe will always haunt me. The first is that my brother was thin. He wasn't thin when I saw him just after Christmas. I remembered him at his bodybuilt zenith, but that wasn't the reality. The second is that he'd left the lights on in the Hall at night. He must have been scared to have done that, just as when we tried to keep the ghosts at bay with our light on in the night at Slade Hooton Hall.

My poor darling little brother.

•

Then I found out something else surprising – even shocking. It wasn't until July 2017 that the Church of England Synod changed its policy to allow the bodies of suicide victims to be buried within the main churchyard. Before that it was left to the discretion of the individual vicar. Some of those bodies in the past were buried to the north of the churchyard. If you look at old churchyards, you might observe some unmarked, but surely deeply mourned graves in a northern, thus colder, position. I think back to the time when my father, and the vicar, would have had to wrestle with this outdated, unkind, inhumane policy and how they each would have desperately wanted, in different ways, for David to be found not to have taken his life. A further motivation for my father to seek to prove to the outside world that David was not stained with the stigma of suicide and to convince himself of the rightness of his quest. He must have had to believe it himself and he stuck to his version. I never heard Dad say anything different while he was alive.

Chapter 34

26th January 2020

I tracked down Brian Lett, the young barrister at the time who had helped my father appeal against the original coroner's verdict of suicide. He became a QC in 2008. Only ten per cent of all barristers (a total of about 1700) make it to the top echelons of being a QC, or Queen's Counsel. He is now based in Wiltshire and Tuscany and has written several books on military history, including one on the secrets behind James Bond, titled *Ian Fleming and SOE's Operation Postmaster: The untold top secret story.*

I contacted him in January 2020. He kindly agreed to speak to me, acknowledging that it must be nearly forty years since we met.

'I hold my cases in a kind of mental filing cabinet and I do remember this case, very sad it was, very sad. The original verdict was plainly wrong and the coroner had caused a lot of suffering for your father.

'I remember the reasons why we knew the case was wrongly decided. There was no actual evidence that your brother had planned to take his life, no note, so the coroner could not have reached the decision he did. I recall something else, to do with the coroner knowing your father, hearing on the grapevine that he had been angry with your brother for not having a job. He may have made his decision more on hearsay than what was in front of the court.

'I barely recall my case of *Barber* in the 1970s, which changed the law, it involved a man falling off a roof. Again, a plainly wrong decision of suicide. That case established the law but I remember your brother's case more clearly. The fact that your brother had so much dog food in his car outside showed his intention to look after the dog for some time.

'The stigma of suicide – it's a terrible thing to happen to your child. Your father was terribly upset, well your mother too, of course. I have four children of my own, it would be awful, unimaginable. I visited your parents at their cottage in Cornwall, with my wife, and they came to visit us, I kept in touch. It felt like such an injustice. It didn't mean that it wasn't suicide but on the evidence before the court the original decision was plainly wrong, and that is what my job was as a lawyer, to show that.'

I find out that Brian Lett worked on the case on a pro bono basis, for free. Barristers' clerks normally negotiate fees in advance, as they would have done here. But Brian Lett did not believe this was right in my brother's case. I check this with him.

'I did not offer to do the case pro bono from the start. My clerk would have never allowed that! He negotiated a fee. I did the case, then notified my clerk that I would not accept a fee for my work. I was sensitive to the enormous sadness surrounding your family, thought the Coroner was wrong, and didn't want to make any money out of putting the verdict right.'

'Thank you, you did a very good job. Sorry, that sounds inadequate, but you did,' I said. My father must have felt that Brian Lett was heaven sent.

I then think a bit more about the coroner. Lieutenant Colonel Henry Thompson (known as Harry) was described by my father to me as a Captain Mainwaring (from *Dad's Army*) lookalike. If I've found the right chap on the internet, it looks as if he had not been to Cambridge, indeed might not have been to any university, which was unusual for a coroner. But was there another reason, or motivation, for the decision weighted against my father – a flawed legal decision, even if the reality of my brother's taking his life was true?

The only other boyfriend of my mother's that I ever heard talk of was a red-headed man called Harry. My grannie confided this to me when she was getting demented but still had enough of her mind to recognise a fact which my mother would have not wanted me to know. When I told my mother this, she blushed and said, 'That's not a subject which I wish to talk about. Your grandmother should never have said anything.'

It is statistically improbable (there must be other redheaded men called Harry …) but strange things did happen in my family. My Aunty Judy clears up this minor mystery. 'Oh, no. That was a Harry from your grandparents' village, Scrooby, from one of the farming families. There might have been a Marcus once, if I remember that rightly but I don't think that Pip had any other boyfriends until she met Geoffrey.'

•

As I was writing this book, early in 2019 a friend asked me if I'd heard the Radio 4 *Woman's Hour* series about family secrets. No, I said. Anyway, I'm not ready to go public about this story yet.

But once the summer has passed, I am. I contact *Woman's Hour* and have a seven-hour radio interview with their skilful interviewer, Jo Morris, who comes back again and again to a question with which I have little past history: 'How did that make you feel?'

My story, now edited to around ten minutes, is set to be broadcast in spring 2020.

Then another question raises itself. Nick Cain. What if he hears me? Will he recognise me? He probably won't, but what if he does? Is he still alive? Could this hurt him, or his family if he has one? Has he buried what happened deep in a box, never intended to see daylight? And what about me? My life has started to find its own level. I am loved, secure, settled. Bringing this story into the public arena seemed like a good idea at the time but I now start worrying about whether it will mess things up again, and shoot me back into the crater which was blasted inside me when David died.

Tim gives me a hug, tells me not to worry. 'Trust your instincts,' he says.

Trusting my gut is the better way, even if it will take me out of my comfort zone here. You can have comfort or courage in life, not both at the same time. Something else I've learned. Sometimes too you need to sit with a decision for a while, waiting to hear the quiet voice inside which will tell you what's right. It's not shouty and you need to be quiet yourself to hear it.

Chapter 35

From time to time over the years since David died, when I visited my parents at the Salt Box, neighbours would update me about what had happened to so and so, who had married, who had children, who was ill or had died. I had gleaned that Nick had married his childhood sweetheart, that they had some years later divorced and after more years she had died but I didn't know anything more than that. If the truth be told (and I did promise you that) I was worried about how Nick's life might have turned out. Our last meeting was so jagged and I was left in no doubt that he never wanted to see me again.

With some nervousness, I look Nick up on the internet. Hardly anything, but he is still shown as being at the same address with his occupation listed as a farmer, and so is a woman, Alex Cain, a few years younger than him. Same surname. Perhaps he has remarried? That sounds positive.

I decide the only thing to do, to get over this shall-I-shan't-I dilemma, is JDI, just do it. Write to Nick Cain. I agonise over what to say. Should I send my love? Too weird. Definitely no kisses, in lower or upper case.

This is what I wrote.

Dear [Nick]

Forgive me writing out of the blue like this. I am sorry in advance if receiving this letter is a shock. I very much hope that this finds you well, healthy and happy.

I wanted to let you know I'm currently writing about my family – and trying to make sense of what happened to David all those years ago (and my father's endeavours to prove what had happened wasn't suicide). Plus also my mother died in December 2017 (after my father had died three years before) and she left a confession on the back of an envelope that she was gay. So, all told, there are a number of secrets to be worked through.

Longer term, I also want to help campaign about the importance of talking (and not holding on to secrets) partly to try and prevent more suicides in future.

I've also recently found some papers about the appeal against the verdict of suicide which my father brought, which has given me more information about what occurred, or at least what came out in the legal case. Some of it was unexpected.

I would ideally like to meet up to talk about what happened if you felt you could, maybe in Devon if that would be better – or somewhere else? It's obviously absolutely up to you whether you would choose to do this. I hope you will. I've put my home number above. Perhaps you could call me?

I had a quick look on the internet and you seem still to be living in Northcote. And have maybe remarried? I really hope things are working out very well for you.

Just to let you know, I had cancer a few years back, now recovered and remarried last year (so at home I'm Helen Rice). I've taken time off from work to do this writing and am thus at least for the next few weeks usually at home.

Sending my very best and warmest wishes.

The letter ends up being sent on Halloween. Ghosts from the past. Perfect timing?

As it's Halloween outside, the children come up our drive to get their end of October sweetie haul and the dogs bark, on edge. 'Trick or treat?' The tiny ghouls and witches who come up to the door, shepherded by their parents, don't look as if they have any tricks in them. But there is an unmistakable chill outside, even if not within. My Sussex house, our home, is like Winnie the Pooh's house, warm in winter and cool in summer.

For a day or two, no phone call. I gave him a landline number. I check the answerphone: not on. Darn it. I switch it to active, then try to forget about it. He probably won't call, anyway.

Sometime after 4 p.m. on Monday 4th November, the home phone rings. I see the first few numbers, it looks like the hospital reminding Tim about his tendon injury check-up.

Sighing, I pick up the handset.

Me: Hello.

Caller: Hello, is that Helen? Is that you?

Me: Yes, it is. Is it…? A pause. The phone line is deathly quiet.

Him: This is Nick Cain. Are you OK?

Chapter 36

Thirty-eight minutes

Me: (catching a breath) Well, yes. I think so. It's you? Well thank you for calling. How are you?

Him: Yes I am. I couldn't believe that you'd get in touch after all these years, Helen. I looked at the envelope. I didn't guess it was you until after I opened it. I wondered about calling. I don't know if I can help, if I know anything you don't. Are you OK?

Me: Sorry it was a shock. It's just that, well, I'm writing and trying to make sense of it and I've found out some extra stuff. Papers. In a brown envelope that my mother hid under her bed. I didn't know some things about David's death – what came out in the appeal against the inquest. I thought, maybe, well, you might want to know as well. It was a long time ago, God, decades, maybe forty years? In the Bullers, where we met last?

Him: Hmm. Yes. I think so, it was … maybe 1983, if I've got that right, Helen?

Me: Yes, sounds about right. Must be.

Him: There're things I remember and then I don't know if I remember the memory of it or what actually happened itself, do you find that? Does that make sense to you, Helen?

      (It's appealing, this way he has of saying your first name, frequently. It brings a listener in close. I'd forgotten that. I steady myself.)

Me: Yes, you're right. It's like every time I remember something, it's like I take it out of a cupboard, in my mind, you know? – and when I put it back it's different. My parents, they're both dead. I couldn't really talk about David properly while they were alive but now I can talk about it, before I forget. I'm trying make sense of it. I realised I wanted to talk with you.

(I'm gabbling. He was talking quickly, too. He is silent briefly.)

Him: It was a shock, well, a surprise, to hear from you but, well, that time's never gone away for me. It's always there. Since I got your letter, Helen, I've been thinking about me and David, what we talked about. He had a hard time at home; me too. Similar. I don't think about him every day, but it might not be far off that.

Me: I worried that you might have hidden things away, kept it all secret. Put it in a box.

Him: No. Nothing like that. I never hid anything. I don't mind talking on the phone. But I don't know if I can help any you more than that.

(He's said that before. He's going to disappear soon.)

Me: Well, there've been a few secrets this end. My dad ...

Him: Geoffrey, was it? I think I remember your dad's name, I can't remember your Mum's.

Me: Yes he is – well, was – Geoffrey. And my mum's Monica. They're both dead now. My dad died in 2014. I could never talk with him about David's suicide. I thought that's his way of getting through. I didn't think he would have been able to take it if I'd told him, you know, what you knew, we knew.

Him: We have to get by how we can. I think you did the right thing.

Me: Thank you. (Pause.) I've found these papers in an old brown envelope. Nick, David actually bought the gun. From a gun shop in Sheffield. I didn't think he had. I thought he'd found it at the house, you know, so it was more of an impulse thing, like in the moment.

Him: I thought that, too. (Another brief pause.) Do you remember we were together in Derbyshire when the suicide verdict came through? We'd gone away for a weekend? At least that's how I remember it. We talked about it more then.

Me: Were we? Maybe I'd blocked that. There are gaps. When Mum died in 2017, before Christmas, I thought at last that I could start talking about what had really happened, rather than their version of it. Then she kind of trumped it with her own confession.

Him: That she was gay? Like you said in your letter.
(We both laugh, it is surreal, and it's good to hear him laugh. His laugh is free, salt air.)

Me: Yes.

Him: Well that doesn't matter so much, especially these days, does it? Did you find out if she had, like, relationships in the marriage that you didn't know about?

Me: Yes, well, probably. She had a relationship for over four years with a woman before she married. I don't know if my dad knew. But then again he must have? I knew something didn't make sense when I was little but not what. After I found out, I talked to one of my mother's lovers, I'd known her as a family friend. I got to know more. Maybe too much.

Him: I'm sorry. Difficult. Weird, too. What a lot you've gone through, Helen.
(Another short silence.)

Me: So, tell me how you are?

Him: I got married to Caitlin – maybe you knew that? – after I came back. I thought it was the right thing. But it didn't last.

We didn't have children. She got ill, and it affected her really badly. The last five years together were terrible, she was drinking, I was drinking, the arguing … In the end I had to bring it to a stop. It was about 1995 when we divorced. She died later on. (He pauses.) She never told me she loved me unless I said it first, Helen.

Me: Ouch. That's kind of cold?

Him: There were another couple of women after that, one of them was a real bunny boiler. I didn't know what was going on. It was on, off, more arguing. Someone else too. But it wasn't going well, Helen. I was spinning. Then I met Alex. Everything changed. We met in January and got married in March.

Me: What? That's what, not even three months?

(He laughs again, elated at the memory.)

Him: This time I knew it was right. My heart told me. I'd listened to my head before and that hadn't worked out. It was time for me to listen to my heart. Right from the start I've told Alex everything, all about it, about David, about you, no secrets. We've visited his grave. I go up there myself sometimes. If I'm going through the village and I've got a bit of time, I'll stop off, you know, at the graveyard and go see him.

(Tears spring to my eyes at the thought of him visiting my brother's grave. David was buried in the right place.)

Me: That's good to hear that.

Him: But how are you? Do you have any children? What are you doing now? Can you fill me in on your life, you, what's happening, in about, I don't know, maybe two minutes?

(He laughs again, just how I remembered. Hearing Nick's voice, I miss David more, they are so linked in my mind. But it is good to hear him laugh.)

Me: Ah. Two minutes. If that's all I've got, Nick ... Well, I really didn't think I'd see you again after that night.

(Focus. Two minutes. He could put the phone down.)

Me: It was intense for me when we were together. OK, so what happened after? Well, I went on to be a lawyer. And I didn't marry the man I was with in 1983 but I did marry a lawyer. It lasted nearly twenty-five years, not easy at the end. We got divorced in 2014. He died in 2016, and he was ill before that, too. And I have three children.

(Can I tell him this? I've never heard that Nick had children, won't this be painful? But he makes a reassuring *ahhh* sound, warm, affirming. I press on.)

Me: I remarried, Tim, last year, a lovely, gentle man, who has two daughters. So, we have five children between us, in their twenties, not exactly children. What about you? Tell me more about Alex.

Him: She's great. She's wonderful. (He pauses.) And we have two boys.

Me: You're a father! Oh my God, I can't tell you how happy that makes me feel.

Him: I thought that I'd never be a father, Helen, I'd pretty much given up on that. But after Alex and I got together, we went away to France, and she said 'I want your babies!' Well, I thought that had all passed me by. But then I had this chance. And I said 'Yes!' It's fantastic, Helen. I'm so happy.

Me: I'm glad. I thought you'd be a good dad. And that you're happy with Alex. So healing.

Him: And Alex, she's got two daughters from before; they're in their twenties now. (He pauses, this time longer.) I gave up drinking fifteen years ago, Helen, around the time I met Alex. I don't miss it. I was putting on weight, it wasn't doing me any good. She drinks if she wants to; it doesn't affect me.

Me: That makes me so happy, oh I keep saying that. And hey, well done about the not drinking – and for so long! (I pause.) Did you know David was three times over the drink driving limit when he died?

Him: Ooof. Well I was thinking about that time, Helen, after I got your letter. How David and I talked about suicide and how I'd gone up to Slade Hooton Hall with him a few weeks before he'd died. It was cold there, bitter.

Me: That can't be right, my parents sold that in 1976. Was it maybe Bothamsall Hall?

Him: Where's that? I'd always thought it was Slade Hooton Hall. What's that name?

Me: Bothamsall, near Retford in Nottinghamshire, Nick. That's where he died.

Him: Well it must have been that we went there, maybe it was, with Jimmy too.

Me: And when was it that you last saw him, saw David, I mean?

Him: The last night I'd seen him, Helen. It must have been a Wednesday, in Cornwall.

Me: I think that's right. The vicar said he'd seen you both in the Bullers.

Him: Well I don't remember that, though I'm not saying he didn't. David and I went to the Manor. At Widemouth. And I brought David back home, and dropped him off, and he said, come in for a drink. I said I couldn't. I was working the next day, I had to get some sleep. But if I'd have come in that night? Maybe …

(His voice catches. So that's what he meant about 'that night'.)

Me: I hope you don't blame yourself. You know when someone has made their mind up that they're going to do it, kill themselves, I've read that they can become calculating, like it's a plan. He'd got so distant he could hardly be in the same room as me before I left for the States. That last Christmas was a nightmare. It wasn't your fault, Nick, it wasn't mine. It was his choice. (I pause.) You know, Nick, I felt we kind of saved each other.

Him: Well it was the best of times and the worst of times, that's what I think, when I think back on that time. It defined me, Helen. David died, we, you and me, were together, I left home, I went away to Australia. It changed me, and gave me a point of reference.

Me: Like a compass?

Him: Yes, Helen. Something to judge things against. If ever I've had to make a decision, I go back to that time.

Me: I don't know what I'd have done if … and I'm sorry if I hurt you. I want to do what I can, now, you know, write about what happened. See if I can help other people talk. People have talked to me I think because I've opened up. It paves the way. I'm aiming to walk from Land's End to John O'Groats and have meetings in village halls and things. (Pause.) I'm going to come down soon to Marhamchurch, I need to bury my mum's ashes in the grave. Dad's are there.

Him: I didn't know that. Maybe you're going in the same grave yourself?

      (We both laugh.)

Me: No way. I've got other plans, with Tim.

Him: Well, you write what you want, Helen. It's up to you. It's just that, I don't think I can help you any more. It'd not be right. It's past.

Me: Well then, OK. Whatever's best. I've given you another name in the book. I've done an interview for *Woman's Hour*, you know, on Radio 4? For their next series on secrets, in 2020.

Him: It's all right. Say whatever you want. It's good you're doing this. Who'll play me in the film, who do you think, Helen? (He laughs.)

Me: I'll be holding out for Emma Thompson or maybe Meryl Streep. Couldn't say about you.

●

We say farewells. We have separate paths, our own loves; families to love actively, to protect and take delight in.

Real love is not just a feeling, a noun. It's a verb.

He is safe, he is loved, he is happy, he loves, he has a wife, two stepdaughters, is the father of two sons. Thank God for Alex.

Thank God for Tim. And my children and stepdaughters. Family means so much to me. And how could I forget Bentley and our new cocker spaniel, Pippin.

Close relationships – pets included! – are wonderfully protective factors.

We are lucky.

Chapter 37

31st May 2020

As I write this, my black plastic Dalek looks at me from the left of the desk. He (it is probably a he) has been with me for many years and reminds me of the Doctor Who episode where a Dalek falls over. Inside its tough top, the Doctor discovers a pathetic grey mass, pleading for life. We are all vulnerable, underneath.

I look out of my writing room window (still bloody lucky) towards the South Downs, a view I fell in love with even before seeing this sunlit, albeit neglected, house which is now our home. I see the field behind the house, with the land sweeping up towards Telegraph Hill behind. The hill endlessly fascinates me, with its shifting patterns of green and brown, gleaming under sun or wrapped around with mists and rain. I love to walk and look up at that hill every day. It grounds me.

In this field, where most often polo ponies are turned out to rest, before and after the summer polo season, unusually there are six ex-racehorses, five years old mostly, who did not take to racing and need to find another job in life. Horses always gladden the landscape. Did you know that up to ninety per cent of racehorses are affected by gastric ulcers? Too much adrenaline, too much pressure. These horses in the field, all different colours of bay, are the self-preservationists: the ones, you could argue, with sense. For the first few weeks they are here, they follow each other around as though in a trance, their hooves making a track, like a ring, in the field, about eighty metres long. As the weeks go by, in the safety of their herd, in this peaceful field, they pace their track less, relax more. This morning they were all lying down in the field, quite chilled. I have never seen such a phenomenon before. Can they really have been reliving walking the paddock before a race, walking out their trauma until they too can let it go?

Stranger things are happening this year. The human world has changed completely, locked down, fighting a virus, a version of flu, which has no known vaccine or cure. The natural world has never looked more beautiful, with clear skies, filled with sunlight and bird-song: there are fountains of chirruping goldfinches outside, more sparrows than we've seen for years, and the dawn chorus sounds sublime. Humans, many humans on our planet, seem to be realising what really matters.

My writing room, March 2020

Today, 31st May 2020, which also happens to be a Sunday, is the day that my brother would have been sixty, if he had lived. It is the day on which we'd planned to bury my mother's ashes in his grave, so that they would all three be together, but we have had to postpone this, due to lockdown restrictions. This one decision, set against the thousands of terrible decisions that people have had to make about the health, wellbeing, lives – and sadly deaths – of their loved ones, seems insignificant.

To mark this day in another way, Tim and I have joined the Self-Isolation Choir to sing Handel's *Messiah*. Nearly four thousand singers, all in our own rooms and homes, are joining together with a recorded orchestra and soloists conducted by Ben England to sing out this extraordinary sacred oratorio, for which Beethoven said of Handel, 'I would uncover my head and kneel down at his tomb'. Jesus Christ has been named as one of history's most famous suicides, but that's a question too hard for me to judge. In some shape or form, the *Messiah* seems relevant and appropriate, and I know that when I sing the magical 'Hallelujah Chorus', I'll be wearing my mother's flashing opal ring, for she loved classical music, and I shall cry again.

Everyone is unique. This is not a 'how to' book, simply a 'what happened' endeavour. This work is enough now, and I shall soon be letting this book go on its own journey. I have tried when writing it to find some answers for myself about how and maybe why my brother died – sometimes uncovering unexpected further questions, for which there are no answers. I am willing to leave them as they are. I live a life with meaning nowadays, and am more than content.

And if this self could have gone back to my Christmas 1980 self to give some advice? For many years there was just one bit of advice I would have liked to give my past self, for reasons which I'm sure you will figure out, probably better than me.

Don't catch that plane to New York.

I am letting that go now, too. What is past is past, it is what it is. Even if my future self had managed to persuade my past self (certainly no given), that would have wrongly placed me in the middle: not only being able to influence people (which we all do all the time) but also bearing the brunt of responsibility for others.

It was not my fault that David took his life, nor my responsibility. It was ultimately no one else's but David's. We have choices in life that we make as individuals, not just in our roles in relation to other people. David cast away the potential of all his future possible selves, which is a tragedy, but not one to make everyone else's lives tragic for ever.

We, the still living, have our presents and our futures, to develop them as we can and will. That is our responsibility. And, if we dare to open ourselves up to the possibility, our joy.

Chapter 38

We are nearly at the end of the story, this story that has taken me almost forty years to finish. The story of what happened to David; the fulfilment of my promise.

At the beginning of this book, I said I thought you'd probably be able to figure out more of this than I have; to identify more of the factors contributing to my little brother taking his life.

I have come up with twelve: not a scientific process, but it's my way of making sense of why.

If you think there are others, I'd love to hear from you. Or – maybe much more importantly – if you'd like to join me in the mission to grow a climate of tolerance and talking, and stop other people from doing what he did. Every suicide is a tragic loss of a life: let's see what we can do to stem the agony in future and reduce those numbers.

Isolation. David was not only alone, but also lonely. According to Peter Fonagy of the Anna Freud Centre, isolation is the key factor in deaths among all people right across the world: simply put, if you live alone, you are more likely to die younger. Yes, he took his own life: being isolated increased the chances. David had left the lights on in Bothamsall Hall for the last nights before he died. That makes me weep. He must have been scared. Once he no longer had Cleo's company (dogs are a huge source of love for people living on their own) there was probably nothing left to stop him.

Means. Somehow, David managed to scrape together the £46 needed to buy a shotgun, and to make a convincing forgery of a shotgun certificate. There are many thousands more suicides in the US where there is easy access to guns. More young men (and others) die from shooting themselves there than the more publicised mass gun shootings. There's a cover-up. It is hard to face the truth that far too many young (and older) people are taking their own lives. Restrictions on guns in the UK quite literally save people. Guns kill people in ninety-five per cent of suicide cases. With other means, eighty per cent of suicide attempts fail.

His age. Suicide is the single biggest killer of men under the age of forty-five in the UK. The brain does not complete its development until we're in our mid-twenties: until then the connections haven't joined together enough to tell us that we are actually *not* immortal. This youthful illusion has been used in the past to send young soldiers over the top in battles which they could never survive. The length of time needed for the brain to mature exacts a high mortal cost on our young males particularly. The rate of suicide amongst women is one third that of men.

Not being accepted and loved for who he was. My family focussed more on what we might look like to the outside world than how we felt inside. David went to a school where my high-achieving father was a local hero. He liked motorbikes, not the law; he wasn't an intellectual giant.

Comparisons are odious. Parents need to take delight in their children. Delight is the best component of any relationship. David felt he was a disappointment, and his rebellion against that led to him taking his own life. We all need to be heroes in our own life journey, and I imagine that David felt the most heroic thing would be to kill himself because he had failed. A form of hara-kiri.

Sins of the fathers (and mothers). My father and mother were who they were because of the way they had been raised, and the same is true of my grandparents and all the generations before that. Traumas in past generations are passed down like a relay until someone stops and asks, 'What happened?' and then listens to the answers.

Closely linked to the factors above is not talking; **secrets.** Talking about the hurt in the story of what happened to you, being listened to, is the first step in healing. The second is for that hurt to be acknowledged, even if that is by someone else.

Without opening up to each other, touching base regularly, keeping our fingers on our own and each other's pulses of life, we lacked buoyancy to manage life's troubles. David's death wish had been signalled for a while, but no one noticed enough. David and I were brought up in an environment where secrecy thrived, although we didn't even know we knew that, and we were suffocated by it.

Lack of community. My parents' lives as rolling stones meant that we never really had enough time in any one place to develop a close sense of community: roots. The move to Slade Hooton, to fulfil my father's dream, placed major pressures on our family, emotional and financial. We might perhaps have looked like the perfect family from the outside, we put on a good show, but inside we were all a little lost, disconnected. I continue to believe that if we had never left Tickhill, David would not have died. The move away from that family home and our busy family life in a lovely, large village gives me a pang even now.

Inner beliefs. He'd decided not to live beyond the age of twenty, and that must have formed a core inner belief, a lethal promise he intended to keep. I wish I had known that, although whether I was ever equipped to do anything about it, I doubt. He just didn't like the physicality of bodily life – for example he hated pooing. And he did not want to get old.

Planning. Once someone has determined on a suicide plan, it's harder to stop them. Remember this. They can become quite calculating about achieving it, and can even appear happier. David had taken out the last six weeks' pages from his diary to cover his tracks. The 'pact' that I had pictured David making with his best friend had more to do with my imagination than reality, but suicide can also, sadly, be catching.

The lack of an intimate, close relationship. His relationship with his parents, my father in particular, was difficult; and it was difficult with me latterly because I bought in to the family story that we needed to make David do something with his life, rather than be gentle and listen and support him. If he'd had a partner with whom he was happy, that would have been such a protective factor and could have made all the difference. But we tend to attract what we give out and I don't think that David was in a place to have a good, mutually supportive relationship. He was not yet mature enough.

Alcohol. David was drunk when he died. Alcohol has a strong link with most suicides. And that's not just the alcohol in the body at the time of death: alcohol and other mind-altering substances wear away at your mind's ability to control your life, undermining your agency.

Alcohol is a dangerous drug. Realising that when writing this book left me feeling I had no option but to give it up and embrace sobriety. At the time of writing, I've passed a milestone of six months sober. Taking it one day at a time. I'm not promising I'll give it up forever; however the health benefits, good sleep especially, are amazing.

And it's not just alcohol which is toxic. **Toxic masculinity** kills the genuine spirit in men, and hurts women pretty badly too. David was a sweet, funny boy who felt he had to turn himself into the Incredible Hulk to get through life. Losing his hair before he was twenty-one affected him. His go-to place of anger, an emotion which often hides grief – the unacceptability of feelings *other* than anger – made him take his life. As a culture we must become more open, caring, accepting of difference. All the colours of the rainbow, like my mother's opal ring. Otherwise we'll all be colluding in a tragic loss: not only of human lives, but also of the joy of life.

Afterword

As I wrote this book, four central characters shone in the spotlights: my mother, my father, my brother and, because he and his best friend were close, Nick Cain. Plus me. Everyone else faded into the shadows, becoming more Greek chorus than anything else.

If life is one big jigsaw puzzle, you only get to pick a few pieces – maybe part of a border or corner – when you write a memoir, which will necessarily cover less than 0.001 per cent of a life lived. Most of what I wrote didn't make it through the editing process. David's friends, my other loves, the friends in our lives, my first husband, our amazing children and stepchildren (my bonus daughters), all their partners, my tribe of sisters, my family (oh Lordy, even choosing the order of this list is too hard), Grannie and Aunty Judy, who probably helped me get by better than anyone at times – none became major characters. I also didn't get to write about other loves: dogs, horses, cats, and books too (if you wonder why some animals featured and some humans didn't, you might not yet fully know their extraordinary healing power). And my legal work, a huge passion, seeking with other like-minded souls to shift the focus from war to peace in family practice, developing a family-centred approach through talking solutions.

If you loved or love me and are reading this and wondering why you didn't feature, it's not just about protecting you. My focus was on meeting my promise to tell the story of my brother's twenty years of life and how it ended. They say it takes you the rest of your life to figure out what happened in the first twenty years. And then because my mother made her confession, I had to write about that too. Realising that my mother felt she had to keep the deep velvety core of herself secret for nearly all of her life widened my eyes and opened my heart to how much people carry and at what cost. I hope that times will be kinder in future, that revelations of self might be birthed more easily.

The part of this book which relates to my mother's posthumous confession is briefer, although the acreage of words I wrote about my mother, and had to discard, was far longer. My mother was more extraordinary than I've been able to credit her for in this book. My father was funnier, kinder and more generous. Being around the two of them was, for many people, a life-enhancing experience, which it's hard to capture now. David's death snatched away so much life.

Somewhat to my – and, I bet, his – surprise, my brother's best friend whom I have called Nick Cain took up far more scenes in this book than I expected. You never know what will come out when you start writing on a blank page. Perhaps I needed to write more about that love story as so much of the story in my head is about the power of love and healing.

I wrote scenes which I remembered clearly, others that I distantly remembered, and I novelised some other scenes in order to explain things better. I take full responsibility for those. I have given different names for the vicar, whose long conversations with my father I was only a brief part of, Evelyn, Maud and others who may wish to keep their privacy.

As I'm finishing this book, it seems to me that most men still do not share their true selves much, except perhaps to their partner or best friend if they have one. I had lost my brother long before he actually died. Back in 1981, 'Nick' helped me connect back with him. In writing this book out of me, more pieces of the jigsaw came together. The day 'Nick' called me to tell me he didn't mind what I wrote, that he was really happy, married to a beautiful woman he loves and with his own sons and stepdaughters was a wonderful day. I wish them every good thing they would wish for themselves.

And so why, in the end, have I written this book? Because I've found that when I open up about the effect these secrets had on me and those around me, my family, it seems to help those who listen to open up about burdens they have in their lives. I want to do my part in helping to lift the dark burdens of shame, fault and blame that we each individually need to shed, to come out into the light where we can gain our peace. By talking, walking, and connecting. That's my vibe anyway, these days.

In 2023 Tim and I will be walking the length of the country with Pippin (who recently had a planned litter of golden puppies born on 1st September 2020). Our walk from Land's End to John O'Groats will be to fundraise for charities helping people to talk, including Samaritans.

Samaritans' vision is that fewer people die by suicide, recognising that every life lost to suicide is a tragedy. We plan to organise talks along the way – we're thinking of calling it the Silver Lining tour – to encourage other people to talk and connect. Maybe we'll see you? For more information on this and other projects, please visit my website. There are some more photos there and out-takes of chapters I haven't been able to fit in, by the way. I'd love to hear from you.

That's enough for now. I suspect this wasn't an easy read for you. I am sorry if it has been tough going, and I hope it has helped in some way. The last few weeks of writing this book I have felt almost possessed by it; it woke me up at night to tell me which bit needed to go in where. Weird. I am in a hurry now to finish. I want to send it out into the world because I dare to hope that it might enhance a life, even save a life, or lives. If it does that, it will all have been worth it.

Please talk, connect, communicate, walk, look after yourselves really well. Do whatever you need to do, to make your life sing again. Step into the light, stay alive, set your face towards your hopes, desires and dreams and take a step. And keep going.

Love and light to you all.

Helen Garlick
September 2020

Pippin's golden litter of six show cocker spaniel puppies
born 1st September 2020

Look closely at the present you are constructing:
it should look like the future you are dreaming.
   Alice Walker

A bird sitting on a tree is never afraid of the bough breaking.
Her trust lies not in the bough but in her own wings.
   Unknown

Acknowledgements

I'd like to thank everyone who made this book real, and if I added everyone by name, that would be a super long list, not least because it's taken such a long time. If you helped, I hope you know and thank you. After seeing *Toy Story 4*, I began thinking of this book like Forky, the toy created by the little girl heroine from a thrown-away fork, for all the times I wanted it (it wanted?) to go in the bin and to move on to something more comfortable. I'm glad now I stuck with it and hope that this Forky can toddle off and go do some good in the world.

Tim is my rock who happens also to have been an editor in a previous life (lucky me): I want to thank him for everything, and most of all for listening, endlessly, patiently.

Apart from all the rest of my adored and wonderful family and tribe who read the book with empathy and forbearance, and gave me brilliant support, I'd like to thank specifically:

Sam Boyce, for editing with such empathy, wisdom and her light touch, and Megan James before her who gave me enough confidence with her skilful edit to be able to submit the draft to my publishers. Many thanks to Julia Koppitz and Chris Wold of whitefox for their insight, support and professionalism.

Nicola Freeman (née Bower) who read the draft and gave great feedback, whom I held in my heart and mind as my dream reader.

Gabriela Blandy, my writing coach and all the Write No Matter What creatives: such a great team for cheering on our respective creative endeavours.

My CBC online memoir writing group (under wise Cathy Rentzenbrink's tuition) who helped me learn so much about the craft of writing through the generosity of their feedback. Specifically, Pamela, Benji, Jasmine, the three Angelas, Sarah, Justine, Helen, Rosie, Bob, Maeve, Marina, Joyce, Anna and Jo. Thanks to literary editor Kerry who told me that she really believed in this memoir and my ability to write it.

Brian Lett QC for his insights and everything he has done, much appreciated.

Paul Bower (no relation to Nicola), who helped beautifully with the chapter covering Meatwhistle: maybe we will need to do a prequel covering more fully the Sheffield years in the Seventies. We were lucky to be alive and there at that time.

Matthew Syed and Kathy Weeks and her parents for being the first people outside the family to whom I told the whole story and whose reaction galvanised me into cracking on.

Steve and Christine Carey. Christine was born in the same nursing home as me in Doncaster: their feedback was particularly helpful and informed.

Professor Andrew Rice for his help in deciphering the pathologist's report and overall his sensitivity.

My mate Caroline Fleming (best woman at my second wedding) who took me along to a creative writing weekend at West Dean College which kicked it off, as well as walking endlessly with me over Hampstead Heath to sort out life.

Nicola, Caroline, Paul and I are all ex-Meatwhistlers. No coincidence.

And although they will never read this, Bentley and Pippin for accompanying me on all those walks up and down the lane, uncomplaining, joyful, while I figured things out. Big love.

Helen Garlick writes and speaks about the healing power of talking and connection. Hello! It's better to talk.

Previously a well-known family lawyer/mediator and author of various books and textbooks on family matters, including The Which? Guide to Divorce, Helen has appeared on TV, radio and podcasts. She has worked with thousands of clients to achieve amicable outcomes on separation and trained thousands of lawyers in constructive talking solutions, focusing on the family's best interests at heart. Helen spearheaded collaborative practice training for Resolution (First for Family Law) until 2020 and ran bespoke dispute resolution courses. From 2021 she will co-train with Barbara Mills QC on communication, connection and peaceful conflict resolution.

From Yorkshire, Helen now lives in Sussex on the South Downs with her husband Tim. Mum of three, step mum of two. Surprisingly sober since she stepped back from legal practice to focus on writing (maybe that's no surprise at all), Helen will walk from Land's End to John O'Groats in 2023, fundraising for charities dedicated to suicide prevention and wellbeing, alongside Tim and their dogs Pippin and Ziggy Stardust.

No Place to Lie is her debut memoir.